D0854931

CELEBRATING LIFE

March 17th 2004

Susannah,

Happy St. Patrick's Day.

Love always

Jack

Also by Jonathan Sacks and available from
Continuum

Radical Then, Radical Now
The Dignity of Difference

CELEBRATING LIFE

Chief Rabbi Jonathan Sacks

LONDON • NEW YORK

Continuum
The Tower Building
11 York Road
London SE1 7NX

15 East 26 Street
New York
NY 10010

www.continuumbooks.com

First published in 2000 by Fount, an imprint of HarperCollins*Publishers*
This edition published in 2003 by Continuum

Copyright © 2000 Jonathan Sacks

All rights reserved. No part of this publication may be reproduced or
transmitted in any form or by any means, electronic or mechanical, including
photocopying, recording, or any information storage or retrieval system,
without prior permission in writing from the publishers.

British Library Cataloguing-in-Publication Data
A catalogue record for this book is available from the British Library.

ISBN 0-8264-7337-7 (PB)

Printed and bound in Great Britain by Antony Rowe Ltd, Chippenham, Wilts

Contents

Foreword by Ruth Gledhill   ix
Acknowledgements   xiii

1   Staying sane in troubled times   1

Part I – Making a Blessing over Life

2   Not taking life for granted   7
3   Live long, live well   10
4   Giving thanks   14
5   Saved by a grape   17
6   What makes the good news, news   20
7   Letting the blessings catch up   23

Part II – Affirmations in Unexpected Places

8   The good news file   29
9   Failure   32
10   God's script   35
11   Humour and humanity   37
12   Time out   40
13   The fly and the fly-bottle   42

Part III – Where Happiness Lives

14   Having it all   47
15   A lesson in happiness   50

16 The third domain   53
17 Faith lost   56
18 Faith found   59
19 The art of happiness   62

Part IV – Finding God

20 The face of the personal   67
21 The mirror of God   70
22 The voice of silence   73
23 Listening   76
24 A question of faith   79
25 Where we let Him in   82

Part V – Faith in the Family

26 Faith is a marriage   87
27 Love in a loveless world   90
28 Fractured families   93
29 C   96
30 Learning to love   99
31 Being a parent   102
32 What we give our children   105

Part VI – The Moral Voice

33 Our creation   109
34 The moral maze   112
35 Values we share   115
36 Can we make moral judgements?   119
37 The hardest word to hear   122
38 Civility   124
39 Confidences   126
40 Rights and duties   129

Part VII – Communities of Faith

41 Community   135
42 Trust and the Prisoner's Dilemma   138
43 Bowling alone   141
44 Turning strangers into friends   144
45 Where they know my name   147

Part VIII – Faith and Friendship

46 The dignity of difference   153
47 A new way   156
48 Who best values others?   159
49 When we cannot worship together   161
50 Remembering Sir Isaiah   163
51 Cardinal Hume   165

Part IX – From Optimism to Hope

52 Losing our way   171
53 Sifting hope from ashes   174
54 Telling the time   177
55 When civilizations grow old   181
56 Surviving change   184
57 The Tabernacle   187
58 Faith: the undiscovered country   190

Foreword

The Chief Rabbi, Dr Jonathan Sacks, is a powerful and moving writer, which is why he was the first choice of *The Times* when it came to selecting four regular contributors to the 'Credo' column which appears in the Saturday edition of the newspaper on the 'Faith' page. This book, a touching collection of columns derived but not reproduced from his 'Credo' contributions, is one result.

Few religious figures of such prominence are prepared to enter into the demanding relationship of being a regular columnist with the secular press but to our delight, Dr Sacks agreed to write monthly for us. Not only that, but he has never once complained about the cutting and amending that takes place to his articles during the sub-editing process. He did not even object on the occasion when, to make our life easier, he supplied two columns at once, and they were accidentally subbed down to one, losing most of the sense and meaning thereby. If only every freelance contributor were so understanding.

We need people like Dr Sacks in our newspaper, and not only because he never complains. Peter Stothard, editor of *The Times*, says:

> I was always struck by the American analyses that one of the biggest gaps between newspaper readers and newspaper writers was the extent to which newspaper readers were

more likely to be interested in religion than their writers were. As a newspaper we try to have a balance of writers to reflect the world we are writing for. But it is in the nature of people who write for newspapers that few of them will have religious beliefs. Therefore to some extent we have to do slightly more than we would otherwise to redress that balance.

One of the reasons for having the 'Faith' Page and the 'Credo' column is so we can use outside contributors to bring the balance of the paper in line with the balance of the readers.

Dr Sacks' own experiences suggest that, although an establishment figure within and outside the Jewish community, he not infrequently finds himself up against his own establishment when seeking or encouraging change. Some of his columns reflect this. His personal meditations on the resulting experiences can be applied to circumstances we have all faced, whether as individuals or as belonging to an institution.

'I never like to think of us as an establishment newspaper as that suggests we are with the establishment and against our readers,' says Stothard:

The experience of *The Times* in the 1930s when it was an establishment noticeboard but not close to the instincts of the people leads to the conclusion that *The Times* is always best when it is with the people, joshing against the establishment rather than with the establishment, deceiving the people. My instinct is to draw more on the nineteenth-century populist *Times* than the establishment *Times* of the 1930s. Obviously we are a British institution. The Church of England is another such institution which we take a strong interest in. It has a lot of the same problems we have in terms of adaptation to the changing world. But our readers have a strong interest in it, which is why we give it strong coverage.

It is similar for Dr Sacks in his business, the business of faith. 'Faith is at its best when it becomes a counter-cultural force; when it has no power, only influence; no authority except what it earns,' he says.

It is when writing about his personal difficulties, though, that Dr Sacks is most moving. Figures at the head of institutions can easily become icons for some, while at the same time turning into easy targets for others, for the iconoclasts. Rarely can such occasions be isolated from their personal context, even if the individual concerned cannot at the time, for reasons of political and personal integrity, depict the full context which can shed light on events which appear otherwise inexplicable.

Dr Sacks has, during his time as Chief Rabbi, endured various struggles within his own community which have spilled over into the secular world. Here he writes obliquely of the background to one such conflict, a series of events that in fact provided the inspiration for this book. Badly affected by the death of his father, he went through one of the most difficult periods of his life. 'I made mistakes, and being a public figure, I suffered for them. For two years I felt as if I were drowning,' he says.

Many readers will surely identify with this. I was reminded of a particular trauma in my own past, to which I often apply the phrase: 'I tried to drown my problems, but my problems learned to swim.' Dr Sacks describes how he did indeed go swimming, got out of his depth and lost consciousness. A stranger rescued him, and placed him at the foot of his wife. He never discovered the stranger's name but this brush with death has made every day, for him, a celebration, no matter what difficulties it may contain.

This book is about survival, and about faith that survival is possible. It is about human dignity and the possibility that happiness can be had by all, if only we can open our eyes and believe.

RUTH GLEDHILL

Acknowledgements

This book had its origins in the 'Credo' columns I write for *The Times*. It was my way of thanking its editor, Peter Stothard, deputy editor Michael Gove and religious correspondent Ruth Gledhill for giving faith its voice and space each week.

I first planned it as a collection of those pieces, but soon realized that to give the book coherence I would have to write them afresh, which is what I have done. Less than a fifth of the material has appeared in print before. I have tried, though, to keep to the format of short meditations because of the challenges this poses to say serious things simply and briefly. (I love the comment of one Oxford academic about another who writes long and difficult books: 'On the surface, he's profound. But deep down, he's superficial!')

My thanks to Louise Greenberg, my literary agent, and to Kathy Dyke and colleagues at HarperCollins. I could not have asked for more delightful and professional assistance. I owe, also, a special debt to my wife Elaine and our daughters Dina and Gila, who read the book as I was writing it, said they loved it and then persuaded me to keep rewriting until I got it right. In large measure, this book is theirs. It is about the joy we have found together and what helped us find it.

The person, though, to whom I owe most on this occasion is my mother, who for some years now has been asking me, please, to write a book she can understand! This is my response to her request.

To me, she has been a constant inspiration. I was once asked by an interviewer who the formative influences on my life were. I replied, 'My late father, who was always prepared to lose a friend rather than compromise a principle, and my mother, who kept all the friends my father lost.' By her example she taught me and my brothers what other, more overtly religious people sometimes forget: that having faith in God means having faith in other people, and that the measure of our righteousness lies in how many people we value, not in how many we condemn. Still active in her eighties, visiting the sick, doing acts of kindness and finding happiness in unexpected places, she has been, for me, a living role model for celebrating life by enhancing the lives of others, and this book is my way of saying 'thank you' to her.

Staying sane in troubled times

'More than at any time in history, mankind faces a crossroad. One path leads to despair and utter hopelessness, the other to total extinction. Let us pray that we have the wisdom to choose correctly.' Thus Woody Allen on the state of our time.

I like jokes because they are unserious ways of saying serious things. They get past our defences. What we can laugh at, we can face. What we cannot laugh at, we often deny. There is little doubt that something has gone wrong among the many things that have gone right in today's world. We can say what it is. In pursuit of progress, we are losing the script. Our world is moving at breakneck speed, but we are not quite sure where we are going. We are living in a transitional age, and continuous change is among the hardest things for human beings to bear. Small wonder that ours has been called the 'age of anxiety' or, in the title of Francis Fukuyama's latest book, *The Great Disruption*. There are times when we feel like the fabled Russian politician who, getting up to address his fellow parliamentarians, began his speech by saying, 'Friends, yesterday we stood on the edge of the abyss, but today we have taken a great step forward!'

We can diagnose precisely where the trouble lies. The American Declaration of Independence summarized the aims of society as 'life, liberty and the pursuit of happiness'. In the liberal democracies of the West we have done well on life and liberty, but happiness has proved elusive. Despite huge increases in living standards and life expectancy, survey after survey shows that we are no happier than our parents were a generation ago, and our children are even less so. A 1996 *Wall Street Journal* poll found that 60 per cent of those questioned no longer expect their children's lives to be better than their own. In 1993, a survey of American schoolchildren showed that 87 per cent believed that 'most other kids' were depressed and 63 per cent said that most of their friends had considered suicide at one time or another. Another poll in the same year, this time of young adults, found that only 21 per cent believed that they stood a good chance of 'achieving a good life', down from 41 per cent 15 years earlier. This is immensely significant. It spells the loss of an idea that has dominated the West for three centuries – progress, the idea that the human story is one of continuous advance. Ours is the first generation in centuries not to believe that the future will be better than the past.

We can even say why. The past half century has seen the dominance of two immensely powerful institutions, the state and the market. Between them they were thought to be capable of solving most human problems. The great political debate between right and left was which to favour. The left preferred the state, the right the market. The 'third way' that emerged in the 1990s preferred a mixture, a partnership between the two. Search for happiness, though, and you will find it in neither. Happiness is about what we have; the market concentrates on what we do not have. Happiness is about the good we do; government is about the good we pay others to do. A world in which there were only states and markets would be efficient. It would also be a world without happiness.

It has also been an age in which we have turned to scientists – geneticists, neurophysiologists and sociobiologists – to explain the human condition. Science is an immensely powerful tool in understanding nature, but a very weak instrument in understanding *human* nature. To put it more precisely, it systematically misunderstands who and what we are. Science speaks of causes but not purposes. It understands events caused by things in the past, but not acts and decisions motivated by a vision of the future. It is good at dealing with the body. It is out of its depth in dealing with the mind, or what an earlier age called the soul. It has little to say about the ideals that give meaning to a life. Faced with depression, a scientist prescribes Prozac. Drugs cannot yield happiness, however. At most they can tranquillize the pain.

Happiness is not far away. It is here, but first we have to know how to look. I wrote this book out of just such an experience. It had been one of the most difficult periods in my life. I watched my father die, and his loss affected me badly. I made mistakes and, being a public figure, I suffered for them. For two years I felt as if I were drowning. It was then that I remembered something I had learned long ago – that you do not need drugs or therapy to cure depression, though these surely help many people. There is no problem that you cannot think yourself out of, but it needs a special kind of thought. It needs the ability to reframe, to see things differently, to alter perspective, sometimes even to turn the mental picture upside down. That, classically, was one of the great gifts of the religious vision. It does not show you something new. It shows you the things you have seen all along but never noticed. That is all you need. It is what allows you, in C. S. Lewis's lovely phrase, to be 'surprised by joy'.

Our culture has given us a very selective vision, one that renders invisible much of what is around us. As a result it makes joy, exhilaration, the 'good life', unnecessarily hard to find. In these meditations, I have tried to say what happiness is, how we make it, how we lose it, and how we sometimes walk past it without recognizing it. We miss it by looking in the wrong places. In consuming, as if it were something we could buy. In leisure, as if it were somewhere we could escape. In changes of relationship and lifestyle, as if it were just over the horizon. It is not somewhere else; it is where we are. It is not something we do not yet have; we already possess it. It is not fantasy; it is reality experienced in a certain way. Happiness is a close relative of faith. Not faith narrowly conceived as religious doctrine – that has a place, but it is not my subject here – but faith as a form of attention, a way of not taking things for granted, of giving thanks; faith as the courage to make and keep commitments, out of which relationships of trust are born.

Roberto Benigni made a film about the Holocaust and called it *Life is Beautiful*. I do not know if I could go that far, but there was in that title an astonishing affirmation. It had to do with the power of the human spirit to defeat tragedy by celebrating life in the midst of suffering. Life is beautiful if we open our eyes. This book is about how I learned to open mine.

PART I

Making a Blessing over Life

2

Not taking life for granted

It happened on our honeymoon. We had decided to go to Switzerland. I had always wanted to see the mountains, to climb high and breathe the chill air. It was beautiful in theory, and it was no less lovely when we arrived. The valley was bathed in light. The mountains looked down on us in majesty.

The next day we got ourselves ready for a climb and went outside. The mountains had disappeared! The one thing we had not reckoned on had happened. It was raining. The mountains had retreated behind a covering of low cloud. Gamely, for a few days, we climbed, wrapped in mist and dampness through which nothing could be seen. Eventually we decided it was too miserable. 'Let's try somewhere else,' we said. So we hitchhiked down to Italy and there we found the sun.

We stayed in a little coastal town called Paestum, an ancient place with some fine Roman ruins. And the sea. Rarely had it seemed more inviting than just then, after the gloom of Switzerland. The trouble was ... I could not swim. It was not that I had never tried, but somehow I just could not get the hang of it.

As we sat on the beach and looked out across the water, however, I realized that the shore must be sloping very gently indeed. People were far out into the sea and yet the water was only coming up to their knees. It looked safe just to walk out, and so it was. I walked out to where I had seen people standing just a few minutes before and the water gently lapped against my knees. Then I started walking back to the shore. That was when it happened. Within a minute I found myself out of my depth.

How it happened, I am not sure. There must have been a dip in the sand. I had missed it on my way out, but walked straight into it on my way back. I tried to swim. I failed. I kept going under. I looked around for some possible source of rescue. The other people bathing were a long way away – too far to reach me, I thought, too far even to hear. Besides which, we were in Italy. As I went under for the fifth time, I remember thinking two thoughts: 'What a way to begin a honeymoon!' and 'What's the Italian for "help"?'

It is difficult to recapture the panic I felt. Clearly someone rescued me, or I would not be writing now. At the time, however, it did seem like the end. As far as I can reconstruct that moment in my memory, I had already reconciled myself to drowning when someone, seeing me thrashing about, swam over, took hold of me and brought me to the shore. He deposited me, almost unconscious, at the feet of my wife. I was too shocked to do or say anything. I never found out his name. Somewhere there is someone to whom I owe my life.

It changed my life. For years afterwards, I would wake in the morning conscious of the fact that but for a miracle, I would not be here. Somehow that made everything easier to bear. Our life has had difficult times. It has had moments of crisis. Public life is full of stress and not everyone who lives it has a thick skin. People often ask me, 'How do you bear it?' The answer is simple. That day, on an Italian beach, I learned that life, which I so nearly lost, had been given back to me. It is difficult to feel depressed when you remember fairly constantly that life is a gift.

This is why, every morning, I say with real feeling the traditional Jewish prayer on waking up: 'I thank you, living and everlasting King, for restoring my soul to me in compassion, great is Your faithfulness.' Thank you, God, for giving me back my life.

It was then that I realized something I should have understood long before. Faith is not a complex set of theological propositions. It is simpler and deeper than that. It is about not taking things for granted. It is a sustained discipline of meditation on the miracle of being. 'Not how the world is, but that it is, is the mystical,' said Wittgenstein. Not how we are, but *that* we are, is cause for wonder, and faith is the symphony on that theme.

We are here. We might not have been. Somehow that makes every day a celebration, for at the core of that mystical awareness is the discovery that life itself is the breath of God.

3

Live long, live well

Near the bottom of an inside page, the headline caught my eye. It was a newspaper article headed, 'Faithful live longer'. Intrigued, I read on. It was a report of a study published in the United States by *Demography* magazine. The researchers had taken their data from the 1987 National Health Interview Survey, which studied the health patterns of 28,000 people. They decided to chart their histories to see what made a difference to how long people lived. What they found surprised them. The most significant factor was faith, or at least regular attendance at a place of worship.

This is how the article put it: 'Those who turn to religion in the expectation of enjoying eternal life can also look forward to a few extra years on Earth ... Worshippers who attend a service at least once a week live seven years longer than those who do not.' According to the report, a 20-year-old who went to a religious service once a week could look forward to a life expectancy of 82 years. One who did not would live on average for 75 years. Among certain ethnic groups the difference was even more marked – up to 14 years of extra life.

This was the third of a series of recent reports highlighting the positive effects of faith on health. Within days, a fourth appeared. This one was based on a study of 4,000 elderly people in North Carolina. It showed that those who attended weekly religious services were 46 per cent less likely to die during a

six-year period than those who went less often or not at all. Even
after controlling for other factors that might have affected the
outcome – illness, depression, social connections and health
practices – the difference was still a massive 28 per cent. Putting
together the various findings, it transpires that religious people
have lower blood pressure, less depression, less anxiety and
stronger immune systems.

This set of effects is not unique to religion. Much the same
results emerge for those who stay married. They too suffer from
less depression and stress-related illness and live longer than those
who are divorced or separated. There seems to be something
common at work in the two cases – something to do with the
texture of relationships, the availability of support, the quality of a
life lived with and for others, and the sense of worth we get when
we know we are valued, whether by God, a loving partner, or the
fellow members of a community. Happiness turns out to be
as good for the body as for the soul. Successful marriages and
houses of worship are two places where happiness has a home.

What interests me about these findings is less what they
show than how they are likely to be received. Probably with no
more than mild and fleeting curiosity, is the short answer. It is
one of those cases where a thought experiment helps us to see
what is at stake. What if – instead of faith or marriage – the factor
in question turned out to be a new drug, or a diet, or a physical
fitness routine, or a therapy? Imagine any of these emerging
from controlled clinical tests with the promise of seven added
years of life and a massive reduction in susceptibility to fatal
illness. The impact would be enormous. Just think of the rush
of new books, magazine articles, television programmes and
commercial spin-offs.

It is as if our culture has established ruthless screening
devices. Certain messages get through; others get filtered out.

Those that get through have to do with the body and to a
limited degree the mind. Those that have to do with the soul – at
least in the Judaeo-Christian sense of what binds us to others and
to a transcendent reality – get lost amid the noise. They are not
serious. They are not us. They are not 'where we are at'. This,
I believe, is an error. No culture should close itself off from a
major source of health, energy and wellbeing.

Faith, once the code that governed lives, is now seriously at
odds with the mainstream of our values. Its message has become
angular, countercultural, strange. It suggests that rather than
simply satisfying desires, one of the most important challenges
of life is to know which desires to satisfy. It hints at needs that
cannot be met in the market place, not least the most fundamental human need of all, the need for meaning. It reminds
us that somewhere in the endless cycle of work and leisure,
producing and consuming, we need to make space for exercise of
the soul as well as the body. We need a diet high in ideals as well
as fibre. Living long may not be entirely unconnected with living
well, and living well may turn out to be a matter of establishing
the right connections between us, others and the universe.

So does faith help you live longer? I do not know, but there is
a sentence in the apocryphal book Ecclesiasticus that hints at an
answer. 'Gladness of heart is the life of man, and the rejoicing of a
man is length of days.' Celebration is a psychological affirmation
that has physical dimensions, and celebration is at the heart of
faith. Whether or not it makes us live longer, it lets us live each
day to the full. Faith is about how we live, not how long. But
perhaps that is precisely the point. Happiness is elusive. You do
not find it by pursuing it. Pursuing other things, it finds you –
always provided that you are pursuing the right things.

Faith encodes the long experience of humanity as it has
sought to understand and respond to the mystery of existence. It

helps us to live better, more generously, with less fear and more delight than we might otherwise have done. It teaches us to construct environments that honour the human spirit. It helps us to develop an appetite for life, to cherish the miracle of being, to celebrate in the midst of uncertainty. Perhaps that is its secret, its wisdom and its gift. Faith teaches us to make a blessing over life.

4

Giving thanks

Oliver James' book *Britain on the Couch* tells a depressing story. Quite simply, we have become more depressed. Twenty-five-year-olds today are between three and ten times more likely than their parents to have suffered some form of depressive illness. We have become, in James' phrase, a 'low serotonin society' – serotonin being the chemical register in the brain of general states of wellbeing.

Depressive illness is tragic and needs serious medical attention. James' book, though, raises a larger question. Can there be, he asks, something in our culture that has given rise to this sudden increase? Admittedly, it will not explain individual cases, only trends, but the question is real and has a long history. Just as there can be a physically unhealthy society, so there can be a psychologically unhealthy one.

James argues that part of the blame lies with the chaos of intimate relationships, especially the breakdown of the stable two-parent family. No less important, though, are the kinds of emotions favoured by a commercial, competitive society. 'Advanced capitalism,' he says bluntly, 'makes money out of misery and dissatisfaction.'

Paraded daily before us on our television screens and in our newspapers are images of perfection, people who are more beautiful, thin, clever or attractive than we will ever be. Ours is a culture of artificially created longings. We are invited to resolve the tension by buying this, or wearing that, or going there. Unhappiness is good for business. It just happens to be bad for people.

At this stage, the religious believer wants to protest that it need not be like this at all. It is not a matter of opposing capitalism and all its works. It has, after all, made possible much of what makes life more dignified for more people than ever before. Economic growth and technological progress have allowed us to treat disease, conquer absolute poverty and extend the possibilities of travel and communication. Never before has so much been available to so many. The best cure for nostalgia is to imagine going to the dentist in any previous historical era. There is nothing wrong in celebrating the achievements of advanced societies.

There is, however, one spiritual discipline which religion once gave us and which we still need. It is the simple act of saying 'thank you' to God. There are prayers in which we ask God for the things we do not have, but there are others in which we simply thank God for the things we do have: family, friends, life itself with its counterpoint of pleasure and pain, the sheer exaltation of knowing that we are here when we might not have been. Gratitude, the acknowledgement that what we have is a gift, is one of the most profound religious emotions. It is to the mind what serotonin is to the brain.

To thank God is to know that I do not have less because my neighbour has more. I am not less worthwhile because someone else is more successful. Through prayer I know that I am valued for what I am. I learn to cherish what I have, rather than be diminished by what I do not have. A third-century rabbi put it simply. 'Who is rich?' he asked. Not one who has much, but 'one who rejoices in what he has'.

There is no single route to happiness, just as there is no single cure for depression, but the daily discipline of thanking

God for what we are and what we enjoy is the most ancient form of what is today called 'cognitive therapy'. Making a blessing over life is the best way of turning life into a blessing.

5

Saved by a grape

It was one of those moments when you wish the ground would open and swallow you up.

We had been invited, Elaine and myself, to lunch at 10 Downing Street for the first time. The Prime Minister, John Major, was hosting a small gathering to welcome the then President of the State of Israel, the late Chaim Herzog. We were thrilled to be going.

With some days to go, our office received a phone call. It was 10 Downing Street with an unusual request. Since the Chief Rabbi and the President would require kosher food, and so as not to embarrass us by making us eat differently from others round the table, it had been decided to make the whole lunch kosher. Could we arrange for a caterer? Of course we could. I was immensely moved. Sometimes I wish we Jews were as sensitive to one another as others are to us.

The next day we received another call. It was 10 Downing Street again. Would the Chief Rabbi please say grace at the lunch? He would be delighted to, my Executive Director replied. There was a pause, then a hesitant voice continued, 'Do you think it could be a short grace? The Prime Minister's schedule that day is rather tight.' (It turned out that this was the day on which, immediately after the lunch, John Major went to the House of Commons to announce the break-up of the marriage between Prince Charles and Princess Diana.)

There is such a thing as a short grace in Judaism, although the details are somewhat technical. It involves using something called *mezonot* bread – bread made in an unusual way – which does not require us to perform the ritual washing of hands before the meal or the full grace afterwards. We said we would arrange it.

The day arrived. It was a splendid gathering. As well as the President, there were several members of the Israeli Cabinet, together with the British Prime Minister, Foreign Secretary and other distinguished guests. It is hard to explain what it means to be a member of a people for so many centuries deprived of civil rights, and then to be present at such an occasion, in freedom and equality, standing tall. Inwardly I made the blessing thanking God for 'bringing us to this day'.

The guests made their way into the dining room. We took our places at the table. The Prime Minister stood and said, 'I now call on the Chief Rabbi to say grace,' and everyone rose expectantly. It was then that I realized that, just when you think you have explained everything, there is always something you have overlooked.

In Jewish law, to make a blessing, you have to hold the thing over which you are making a blessing. It has to be there, or you cannot bless it. That is why, in a Jewish home, there is always bread on the table at the beginning of the meal. It never occurred to me that this might not be the universal custom.

The table at No 10 was empty. Sixteen people were waiting for me to make a blessing, and there was nothing to make a blessing on. Nor was there anyone to turn to. The waiters had disappeared into the kitchen. The Chef de Protocol had withdrawn. What do you do on such an occasion? I was faced with the choice of saying what, in Jewish law, would have constituted taking God's name in vain, or of disobeying the Prime Minister and remaining silent. Out of nowhere, a diplomatic debacle was in the making.

I was just lifting my eyes towards heaven when my prayer was answered. Halfway down the table was a gold ornament. Someone had decided to adorn it with a bunch of grapes. It was the only item of food in the room. In relief I made a comprehensive blessing that included grapes, and ate one. Honour was saved.

Later, we had a laugh over what had happened. 'Prime Minister,' I said, 'your faith is different from ours. To put it bluntly, you have more faith than we do. You thank God for "that which we are about to receive". After long experience, we prefer to have received it first!'

God sends us messages all the time, usually in code. I think this one was saying, 'Remember what a blessing is.' A blessing is an expression of the miracle of simple things. Making a blessing means recapturing the vision of which William Blake wrote:

To see a world in a grain of sand,
And heaven in a wild flower,
Hold infinity in the palm of your hand,
And eternity in an hour.
(*Auguries of Innocence*, l. 1–4)

I was being reminded that, yes, Prime Ministers and Presidents are important, but so too is a grape. All around us are incarnations of glory, and all it takes to see them is to say a blessing – for the moment, for God's gift, for life.

What makes the good news, news

Once I tried the following experiment. I showed an audience a sheet of white paper, at the centre of which was a black dot, and asked them to tell me what they saw. With only one exception they replied, 'A black dot.' I then pointed out that the dot took up less than one per cent of what they were looking at. They had missed, discounted or ignored the white sheet of paper that gave the black dot its place. As soon as they realized this, we began to understand together why the media so often present a distorted view of the world – why bad news is news, while good news rarely is.

The information that surrounds us daily is all too often a litany of disasters – wars, famines, crashes, crimes, terrorist incidents, public figures suspected of wrongdoing, the clash of politicians, fears about the future. Pleas like that of the broadcaster Martyn Lewis for more balanced reporting tend to fall on stony ground. Those who argue for more good news are often accused of being naïve or sentimental, of wanting to whitewash over the pain, suffering and corruption that prevails in so many parts of the world. One journalist I know defines news as 'something that someone wants to keep out of the papers'. Is that right? Is the world really as bad as it seems?

The simple explanation is that news is like the black spot on white paper. If the paper were black, we would not even see it. Bad news is news precisely because so much of life is good.

Lawbreaking is noteworthy only because the vast majority of people are law-abiding. Corruption hits the headlines only in countries where honesty is the norm. Family breakdown is worth reporting for the simple reason that most people continue to aspire to lifelong marriage as an ideal. What catches our attention is the odd, the discrepant, the out of place. Our senses are predisposed to notice movement, not the things that stay solidly in place. The very fact that bad things are newsworthy is the most telling evidence of the fundamental goodness of our world.

This, for me, is the power and necessity of prayer. There are prayers in which we ask for things, but much of the world's liturgy asks for nothing. It gives thanks for what we are and what there is. Such prayer is more than the expression of a mood, a temporary elation. It is part of sanity itself. Prayers of thanksgiving bring to the foreground what is usually in the background. They are acts of focused attention on the white paper without which we would not notice the black dot. They remind us that without the dominance of kindness we would be indifferent to cruelty. Without faithfulness we would be unmoved by betrayal. Around us everywhere, flooding us with its light, is the dazzling goodness of most of creation – order instead of chaos, diversity not monotony, the brilliant colours and intricacy of the natural world and the hundred acts of human grace for every one of gracelessness.

The majesty of faith is that it teaches us to see what exists, not merely what catches our attention. As animals, we are genetically programmed to see danger, risk, movement, threat. Without this we would not survive. Nonetheless, the very existence of thanksgiving tells us that we are more than just animals. Admittedly there is suffering, poverty, hatred and war. What gives us strength to fight these things, though, is the knowledge that they are not *all* there is. Evil is not the ultimate reality and in this knowledge hope is born and we are lifted beyond the gravitational pull of despair. What makes us human is that we are capable of seeing existence whole, the landscape of beauty that forms the backdrop against which we notice the ugly, the cruel and the unjust. Prayer, not the press, is what makes the good news, news.

Letting the blessings catch up

Rabbi Levi Yitzhak of Berditchev was looking out over the town square. Everywhere he saw people rushing. He called out to one man, 'What are you rushing for?'

The man replied, 'I'm running to make a living.'

Levi Yitzhak said, 'What makes you so sure that your livelihood is in front of you so that you have to rush to catch it up? What if it's behind you? Maybe you should stop and let it catch up with you.'

That story, so telling in the nineteenth century when the incident took place, has become even more true in our time. Ours was supposed to be the age of leisure, yet many people work harder than ever. One parent at work has become, in many cases, two. Too many people I know feel endlessly pressurized, trying to juggle home and work, family and career, ambition and recreation. We run in order to stand still. Often the harder we work, the harder we feel the need to work. We can find ourselves so busy making a living that we never seem to have the time simply to enjoy being alive. When do we stop to let our blessings catch up with us?

This is why holy times are important. For me as a Jew, Friday night around the Sabbath table is the high point of the week. The candles send out their soothing light, and the blessings we make over the wine and special bread remind us that what we have is the gift of God. A Jewish Sabbath is family time.

Husbands sing a song of praise to their wives, taken from the book of Proverbs: 'A woman of strength, who can find? Her worth is above rubies.' Parents bless their children, and together we sing our traditional songs. Those who observe the laws of the day do not work or shop, answer phones or faxes, watch television or use the car. The pressures of the outside world disappear, and life becomes simpler and more serene. In ancient times the Sabbath was a protest against slavery. Today it is an antidote to stress, the most effective I know.

A few years ago a young man came to see me in a state of high anger. His wife by a civil marriage was converting to Judaism so that they could have a Jewish home and children. Our rabbinical court told him that he too would have to practise a religious life. Why should he need to change? he demanded. We spoke, and he went away to reflect. Two years later I officiated at their wedding. They radiated happiness.

A few weeks before the wedding, he came to see me. He wanted to thank me, he said. 'At the time, I was angry. But now I understand that you were right. I used to be a workaholic: I worked seven days a week. Keeping the Sabbath has changed my life. Now I have time for my wife and our child. We have acquired friends, and they too have enriched our lives. Today we are part of a community, which we were not before. One day in seven we have time to celebrate, reflect and give thanks for what we have. The work still gets done, but now I have time for the things that matter. Thank you.'

Rest sets priorities in perspective. Whenever I pass the scene of a car crash I find myself wondering what could have been so important that it was worth risking a life to save a few seconds by running a red light or overtaking on a corner. When life becomes an uninterrupted succession of pressures, we lose the natural rhythms of work and rest, striving and relaxing, creating and enjoying. Sometimes we can travel so fast that we completely miss the view. At regular intervals we need to stop, pause and breathe deeply. Jews used to say that food tastes better on the Sabbath. I think they meant, simply, that pleasures taste better when you have time to let them linger on the tongue. Happiness needs tranquillity. As Rabbi Levi Yitzhak said, it is there right behind us, waiting for us to rest so that it can catch us up.

PART II

Affirmations in Unexpected Places

8

The good news file

Finkelstein, so the story goes, suffers severe pains in his chest and is rushed to the finest hospital in America, Massachusetts General. For seven days he receives treatment there. Then, without explanation, he checks out and has himself transferred to a small, run-down, Jewish hospital in New York's Lower East Side.

The doctor on the ward is intrigued by his decision. 'What was wrong with Massachusetts General? Was it the doctors? Didn't they find out what was wrong with you?'

'The doctors,' replies Finkelstein, 'were outstanding. Geniuses! I can't complain.'

'Was it the nurses? Weren't they attentive enough? Were they distant, cold?'

'The nurses were angels. No, I can't complain.'

'So was it the food? Too little? Too boring? It must have been the food, yes?'

'The meals were wonderful. They tasted of paradise. About the food, I can't complain.'

'So tell me, Mr Finkelstein, why did you leave one of the greatest hospitals in the world and come here?'

Finkelstein gives a big smile and says, 'Because here – here I *can* complain!'

Complaining is fine, so long as we learn not to take it too seriously.

There was a time in my life when I became very low. It seemed as if my world was in pieces. What I was feeling was not yet clinical depression, but I had the sense that it was not far away. I spoke to a friend who was a psychotherapist. Her reply was surprising. 'I know you well enough,' she said, 'to know that you can cure yourself. I'll send you the literature, and leave you to work out how.'

She did. I was particularly struck by those approaches called 'cognitive'. They suggest that what we feel is largely determined by what we think. That made sense. We react to events as we perceive them, not as they are in themselves. If we learn to see them differently – if we 'reframe' them – we can alter our emotional reactions.

For example, I knew of people who saw themselves as failures because they were measuring themselves by the wrong yardstick. The best antidote to this is the Hassidic story about Zusya of Hanipol. When asked why he did not behave with more dignity, he replied, 'When I get to heaven, they won't ask me, "Zusya, why weren't you Moses?" They'll ask me, "Zusya, why weren't you Zusya?"' God does not ask us to be someone else. He asks us to be ourselves.

Then there were others who were devastated by people's opinion of them. When they were criticized, they lost self-confidence. When they were praised, they discounted it, 'threw it away'. They filtered out the good news about themselves and attended only to the bad. They did not realize that all criticism falls into two categories – justified and unjustified. Justified criticism is a learning experience. Through it you grow. Unjustified criticism is someone else's problem, not yours. It may be due to incomprehension, envy or simple negativity, but its cause is something else, not you.

So, thinking hard, I found the answer. I bought a file and put in it a note of all the good things in my life. Whenever something positive happened, I kept a record of it there. Then I put it away in a drawer. Whenever I felt low after that, I went into my study, took out the file and read it slowly, inhaling with each page. It never failed. In the words of the Psalmist, it 'restored my soul'. It helped me to set the bad times in context and remember that, despite the pain, life is good. I call it my 'good news file'. I have taught the principle to others and they tell me it works.

Can't complain? Well, yes, we could – but when we don't, we grow.

9

Failure

It is one of my favourite stories, all the better for being true. A young chemist had been working for some time at developing a new bonding agent, a glue. Eventually the work was complete. He tried it out. It did not stick. What is the use of a glue that does not stick? A failure. Time wasted. Effort spent in vain. Back to the laboratory to try again. So 99 out of 100 people would surely have concluded. The young chemist was the one in 100 who thought differently.

Instead of deciding that his work was a failure, he asked, 'What if it's a success? What if I've discovered a solution? The only thing left to do is to find the problem.' He refused to give up. He kept asking himself, 'What's the use of a glue that doesn't stick?' Eventually he found it. It became a huge commercial success. I use it all the time. The non-sticking glue is used for notepaper you can attach and detach at will. That is how the 'Post-It' pad was born.

I think of that story every time I hear someone write off their own or other people's efforts as a failure. That is not just negative thinking, it is destructive – of confidence, morale, self-respect. More importantly, it is not true, or at least, it is not the best way of seeing things.

Whenever colleagues or friends speak of failure, I tell them what it is like to watch a professional photographer at work. Usually they come to a portrait session armed with several rolls of film. They take 72 exposures in the hope that one will be right – unusual, dramatic, or one that just captures the character of the sitter. If it is, the session has been a success. Any observer who did not understand professional photography might be justified in thinking that one usable outcome set against 71 rejects was, on balance, a failure. He would be wrong. He would simply not have understood the logic of creativity, whether artistic or scientific.

Creation, by its very nature, involves taking risks – the experiment that fails, the attempt that does not quite come off. Each is part of the process that leads to discovery. Each is a learning experience. Analysing why something fails is often one of the most instructive exercises we can undertake. Creativity without failure is like being lifted to the top of a mountain without the climb. It may be fun, but it is not an achievement. 'According to the effort,' said the sages, 'is the reward.'

Moreover, we are not, here, now, in a position to judge success. I think of Moses Maimonides, the great Jewish thinker of the Middle Ages. Late in life he wrote a book. It was, he tells us in one of his letters, written for a single disciple who had doubts about his faith. It took a long time. Maimonides was in those days a physician as well as the leader of his community, and the hours for writing were hard to find. Eventually he completed it and sent it to the young man. From his reply it is clear that it did not work. Perhaps he did not understand it. At any rate it did not answer his questions. It was a failure in Maimonides' lifetime. The name of the book was *The Guide for the Perplexed*, the greatest work of Jewish philosophy ever written.

I think, too, of the first Moses. What would his obituary have been like, written by a contemporary? The evidence is there throughout the books that bear his name. When he intervened on behalf of his people, they complained. He had not made things better, he had made them worse. In Egypt, their burdens were made heavier. Leaving Egypt, they came up against the Red Sea. Crossing the sea, they found a desert. First there was no water, then there was no food. Then the people complained there was no meat. Having given the Israelites the Ten Commandments, Moses found that they had made a golden calf as an idol. Sending spies to prepare their entry into the land of Canaan, they came back and said it was impossible. Every effort Moses made to form a free and holy people collapsed. Nor was he privileged to set foot in the land to which he had spent 40 years travelling. Can a life of failures be a success? Sometimes it can be the greatest life there is.

It took much effort, but eventually I learned that you have to make a blessing over failures too.

10

God's script

It was one of those moments that make you feel part of something so much larger than yourself. It was the summer of 1999. I had been invited to open an international sports competition. The participants were Jewish, part of a global network of youth clubs called Maccabi. For the first time their European gathering was taking place in Scotland. There were well over 1,000 young people from 27 different countries. We began, not with the games themselves, but by celebrating the Sabbath together. It was thrilling to pray, make the blessings and sing the traditional songs in the company of so many – especially given all that has happened to European Jewry this century. For the first time we were joined by participants from East Europe, places like Lithuania, Latvia, Georgia and the Ukraine, where Jewish life was being rekindled after 70 years of suppression under communist rule. This was the Jewish phoenix, communities long dormant coming to life again.

We were in the old town of Stirling with its ancient castle, the place where 'bravehearts' William Wallace and Robert the Bruce fought their famous battles against the English. Along with most of the participants of the sports competition, Elaine and I were staying at the university, one of the loveliest campuses in Britain. I had been there once before, under different circumstances. As the Sabbath began, I told the story.

'Almost exactly 30 years ago, I had just finished university and was applying for my first job. There was a vacancy in the

Philosophy Department of Stirling University, and I applied. It was my first job application. I was invited for interview and I came to this building where we are now. I didn't get the job. I was disappointed, but I went elsewhere and did other things.

'What would have happened if I'd been successful? I wouldn't have become a rabbi. I wouldn't have become Chief Rabbi. And I wouldn't be here now, because the university is on holiday. I would have missed one of the largest gatherings of Jews ever to have come together in Scotland and the privilege of being here with you now. What made it possible for me to be here in Stirling today? The fact that 30 years ago I came to Stirling and was turned down for a job. Until now, that rejection hurt. Now I understand that I was part of a different story. Once in a while God lets us see the script.' It was a moment of closure and disclosure.

There are times when the veil that covers the surface of events lifts, and we catch a glimpse of the larger pattern of which, unknowingly, we have been a part. Tradition calls this Divine providence, and I believe in it. Later events make sense of earlier ones. Bad things turn out to have been necessary steps in an important journey. It may take a long time before we see why and how. In some cases we may never understand, but we do so often enough to have the feeling that we are only co-authors of our story. Another hand is at work, and a larger narrative is taking shape. As Isaac Bashevis Singer put it, 'God is a writer and we are both the heroes and the readers.'

Is this fanciful thinking? It has happened too often for me to doubt. I once wanted to become a Fellow of my college in Cambridge. I had dreams of becoming a university professor. Both these things happened. The strange thing is that they happened years after I had given up academic life, while I was travelling in the opposite direction. I have discovered that God often chooses circuitous routes, but it helps to know that where we are, here, now, is where we need to be.

11

Humour and humanity

Cohen, new in town, goes to the synagogue. Everyone greets him like a long-lost friend. The service is delightful. The cantor sings in tune. There is an air of warmth and welcome. Then they reach the reading of the Torah.

All of a sudden, pandemonium breaks out. Half the congregation stand. Half sit. The half who stand start shouting at the others, 'Ignoramuses! Don't you know that when the Torah is being read you have to stand?'

The other half shout back, 'Heretics! Did no one ever teach you that when the Torah is being read you have to sit?' Eventually the noise subsides and the service ends in peace.

The same thing happens the next week, and the next, until Cohen can stand it no longer. The synagogue does not have a rabbi, so he travels to the nearest town that does and is ushered into his study. The rabbi, aged, bearded, surrounded by learned tomes, asks Cohen what he can do for him. Cohen says, 'Rabbi, I need guidance on a matter of Jewish law. Tell me, when it comes to the reading of the Torah, do we have to stand?'

The rabbi thinks, strokes his beard, shakes his head and says, 'No, that is not the tradition.'

'In that case, during the reading of the Torah, do we have to sit?'

'No,' says the rabbi, 'that is not the tradition.'

'Rabbi,' says Cohen, 'you have to help me here. In my

synagogue, half the congregation stand, half sit, and they start shouting at one another.'

The rabbi smiles, nods and says, 'Yes! That is the tradition.'

I love Jewish humour because it lets us laugh where otherwise we would cry. Jewish life has had its share of pain, but what we can laugh at, we can rise above. It is an assertion of humanity in the face of dehumanizing influences. It is our way of breaking the grip of fears that would otherwise hold us captive. If we can keep our sense of humour, we are not yet prisoners of our situation. Laughing, we defeat despair. Humour is first cousin to hope.

The sociologist Peter Berger calls humour a 'signal of transcendence', by which I think he means something in the human situation that points to something beyond. We are part of nature, but there is a dimension of human consciousness that lies beyond nature. There are aspects of the human spirit that cannot be reduced to physics, neurophysiology, cause and effect. One of them is the ability to understand a joke.

Could a computer have a sense of humour? Probably not. The reason, I guess, is that it has something to do with our ability to reframe, think laterally, shift perspective, see things differently, to affirm the freedom of the mind. Berger sees a connection between humour and religion. 'Laughter,' he says, 'redeems.' A joke is 'a vignette of salvation'. I was talking to a friend about someone we both knew, a great religious leader who had a wonderful sense of humour and also genuine humility. 'He takes God very seriously indeed,' said the friend, 'which saves him from having to take himself seriously at all.'

C. S. Lewis once wrote, 'Human life has always been lived on the edge of a precipice ... Men propound mathematical theorems in beleaguered cities, conduct metaphysical arguments in condemned cells, make jokes on scaffolds, discuss the last new poem while advancing to the walls of Quebec, and comb their hair at Thermopylae.' There is something majestic about a human nature that can detach itself from the immediate and soar into the ultimate. Laughter is the refutation of tragedy. A joke is an opening of freedom in the encircling wall of fate.

'Perhaps,' said the sage, putting down his volume of the Talmud, 'considering all of life's suffering, it would have been better not to have been born. But how many are so lucky? Not one in a thousand!' If we can laugh, we can bear the pain.

12

Time out

I was in hospital recovering from a serious operation. An elderly patient – someone I knew from a neighbouring Jewish community – heard that I was there. He came rushing into my room. I thought he was going to wish me well, or ask about my illness, or swap notes about doctors and nurses. Nothing of the kind. With a huge smile on his face, he produced a volume of the Talmud and said, 'How wonderful to have you here, Rabbi Sacks. Now we can study together!'

What a beautiful Jewish habit that is – the passion for learning, the love of intellectual fellowship, the willingness to seize the moment for a conversation about a religious or philosophical theme. In the *shtetl*, the small townships of Eastern Europe where Jewish life flourished before the Holocaust, when two Jews met, their first reaction would be to say, '*Zog mir a pur verter*' – 'Tell me some words of Torah.' They would share some insight one or other had heard from the town scholar, a novel interpretation of a biblical verse perhaps, or a new perspective on a rabbinical text. For a moment they would forget the poverty and insecurity around them and instead be lifted into a brief, exhilarating flight of the spirit and the mind.

That is why I cherish those rare and lovely pauses for reflection – the 'Credo' columns in *The Times*, or 'Thought for the Day' on the BBC's *Today* programme – which break the otherwise relentless flow of news, reminding us that not everything

immediate is ultimate. Not everything that counts hits the headlines. An old friend of mine who used to take long, long walks
told me that the secret of endurance is to take a five-minute
break every hour. You need to stop once in a while, to breathe,
relax, take in the view. Otherwise you wear yourself out. Perhaps
that is true of life too.

There is nothing inevitable about the way we experience
events around us. We can see life as a series of headlines – loud,
brash, brief and disconnected. Or we can see it the way the
Victorians did – in leisurely, three-volume novels in which virtue
counts and life is part of a story. There are all sorts of alternatives
in between, but our 24-hour news culture tilts the balance too
far in favour of a clamorous present that drowns out the voices of
the past.

One way or another, we need a sense of perspective if we are
not to be overwhelmed by the present. Jonathan Swift once said
that, when we look back on the past, we are amazed that people
fought battles over such trivial things. 'We wonder how men
could be so busy and concerned for things so transitory.' Yet, he
said, we never express the same surprise about our concerns in
the present. What today seems so large to us will one day seem
small to future generations. They too will wonder how, in the
mass of detail, we lost the plot.

This is why a culture needs to find room, in the midst of the
now, for the things that are not now. My elderly fellow patient
was right. Yes, we were in hospital. Yes, we were ill. But for a
moment we could be somewhere else, joining the ancient rabbis
in one of their centuries-old debates, entering the endless argument which is our ongoing conversation with God. Who knows
whether, forgetting our afflictions for a moment, we might not
have experienced that leap of freedom which is the supreme
expression of the human mind?

13

The fly and the fly-bottle

Rabbi ben ('son of') Zoma, a sage of the third century, is one of my favourite wise men. He had a knack of seeing things another way. He would ask, 'Who is honoured?' The conventional answer is someone who receives honour: titles, accolades, praise, acclaim. Not so, he used to say. 'The person who is honoured is the one who honours others.'

Or he would ask, 'Who is strong?' Most people would reply that a strong person is one who can conquer his opponents. No, he would say. 'The strong person is one who can conquer himself.'

Finally he would ask, 'Who is wise?' One who knows more than anyone else? No. 'One who learns from everyone.'

Ben Zoma was the kind of person who would come into a room and see an abstract painting which never looked quite right and say, 'You know what's wrong with that painting? You've hung it upside down.' And he would be right.

Sometimes the most powerful problem-solving device is to ask what would happen if we did the precise opposite of what is expected; if we turned the picture upside down. A man once wrote to Rav Kook, Chief Rabbi of pre-state Israel, saying, 'I loved my son. I gave him everything. And now he has abandoned our faith. What shall I do?'

Rav Kook replied, 'You loved your son before. Now love him even more.' Did this change the son? I do not know, but it surely changed the father.

I think of the biblical Joseph, son of Jacob. As a child he was
envied by his brothers. They plotted to kill him and eventually
sold him into slavery. Many years later, when he had become a
person of power, they feared he would take revenge. He replied
with the words they least expected: 'You intended to harm me,
but God intended it for good.' It is not insignificant that the
book of Genesis draws to a close with this remark. The whole
book is a set of variations on the theme of sibling rivalry. In a
single sentence Joseph showed how to move beyond it. The
unexpected is a formidable tool of conflict resolution.

I think too of the late Anwar Sadat and Yitzhak Rabin, men
who had spent much of their lives waging war. In both cases, late
in life, they asked, 'What if we do the opposite? What if we take
the initiative in making peace?' Both did, and thereby achieved
what they could never have done by battle. They redrew the
political map of the Middle East.

Scientists know that it takes lateral thinking of a high or-
der to solve problems that seem insoluble. On one occasion
Wolfgang Pauli gave a talk on elementary particle physics at
Columbia University. In the audience was one of the greatest
physicists of the twentieth century, Niels Bohr. After the lecture
Pauli said to Bohr, 'You probably think these ideas are crazy.'

'I do,' replied Bohr. 'Unfortunately, they are not crazy
enough.'

Scientific discovery is often a matter of 'paradigm shift',
changing perspectives, looking at phenomena in a totally unexpected way. Seeing things differently opens up avenues where
before every road seemed closed.

No one applied this lesson to tragedy more powerfully than
the late Viktor Frankl, a survivor of Auschwitz who, on the basis
of his experiences there, founded a new school of psychotherapy.
He said that in the camps, they took away everything that made

us human except the one thing that can never be taken away
– the freedom to decide how to respond. Frankl survived by
refusing to see himself as a prisoner. He stayed sane by con-
ducting himself as a free man.

Ben Zoma's principles are all about refusing to be defined
by circumstance. They are about the action that is not reaction.
Our ability to see and do the unexpected is the link between
human creativity and freedom. Wittgenstein once said that his
aim as a philosopher was 'to show the fly the way out of the fly-
bottle'. The fly keeps banging its head against the glass in a vain
attempt to get out. The more it tries, the more it fails, until it
drops in exhaustion. The one thing it forgets to do is to look up.

PART III

Where Happiness Lives

14

Having it all

Poor Kohelet. He was the man who wrote Ecclesiastes. Tradition has long identified him with King Solomon. He was, we recall, the man who had it all and discovered it was not enough. Palaces, gardens, wives, wealth – all promised happiness. None delivered. The more wealth, the more worry. The more knowledge, the more weariness of spirit. In the end all he could say was, 'Meaningless, meaningless, everything is meaningless.' We recognize Kohelet. He is the billionaire with the private jet, the apartment on Fifth Avenue, the holiday home in Cap Ferrat, the Armani suits and the expensive wife, who discovers that it all adds up to less than the sum of the parts. The route to happiness turns out to be harder than taking the waiting out of wanting.

Kohelet forgot something that I discovered by chance. Many years ago I went to visit one of the great religious leaders of the twentieth century, the Lubavitcher Rebbe. As I sat waiting to see him, I began talking to some of his followers. Among other things, they told me this story.

Someone had written to the Rebbe in a state of deep depression. The letter went something like this. 'I would like the Rebbe's help. I wake up each day sad and apprehensive. I can't concentrate. I find it hard to pray. I keep the commandments, but I find no spiritual satisfaction. I go to the synagogue but I feel alone. I begin to wonder what life is about. I need help.'

The Rebbe wrote a brilliant reply that did not use a single word. All he did was this: he circled the first word of every sentence and sent the letter back. The disciple understood. The Rebbe had answered his question and set him on the path to recovery. The ringed word was 'I'.

It is hard to translate a biblical text from classical Hebrew into contemporary English and still preserve the nuances of the original, but Kohelet's problem was the same as that of the letter-writer above. 'I built for myself ... I planted for myself ... I acquired for myself...' In Hebrew the insistence on the first person singular is striking, reiterated, discordant. There is no other book in the Bible that uses the word 'I' so many times as do those first chapters of Ecclesiastes. Kohelet's problem was that he kept thinking about himself. It made him rich, powerful, a great success. As for happiness, though, he did not have a chance. Happiness lives in the realm called Not-I.

There is a lovely story about the great Victorian Anglo-Jew, Sir Moses Montefiore. Montefiore was one of the outstanding figures of the nineteenth century. A close friend of Queen Victoria and knighted by her, he became the first Jew to attain high office in the City of London. He went on to become President of the Board of Deputies of British Jews, in effect the lay leader of the Jewish community, a role he held with distinction for many decades. A wealthy man, he retired at the age of 40 and devoted the rest of his long life – he lived to be 101 – to serving the Jewish people throughout the world as an international diplomat and philanthropist. He built the first almshouses in Jerusalem and the windmill overlooking the Old City. They are still there today. Yemin Moshe, Jerusalem's artists' quarter, is named after him.

Someone once asked him, 'Sir Moses, how much are you worth?' Moses thought for a while and named a figure. The other replied, 'That can't be right. It's a large sum but not large enough. By my calculation you must be worth 10 times that amount.'

The reply Sir Moses gave was moving and wise. 'You didn't ask me how much I own. You asked me how much I'm worth. So I calculated the amount I have given to charity this year, and that is the figure I gave you. You see,' he said, 'we are worth what we are willing to share with others.'

He understood what Kohelet did not. Happiness is not made by what we own. It is what we share.

15

A lesson in happiness

What is happiness? Over the long course of civilization, it has proved as hard to define as to achieve. Aristotle called it an activity of the soul in accordance with virtue. Bentham defined it as the balance of pleasure over pain. Our culture tends to define it as a new car, an exotic holiday, or the latest suit from this year's designer. A car bumper sticker in the United States proclaims, 'The guy with the most toys when he dies wins.' The way we define happiness tells us who we are and in what kind of culture we live.

The greatest lessons in happiness I ever learned came from funerals. As a rabbi I often had to officiate at them, and I hated them. They were distressing moments and they never got any easier. Nothing wears away the raw edge of grief and there is little you can say to a family in the shock of bereavement to ease the pain. Yet nothing taught me more about the meaning of a life.

In my address I had to paint a portrait, one that was true to the person who had died, but one that also summed up what he or she meant to the people who were closest. Talking to the relatives before the funeral, I would begin to see the contours of a life, the things a person had done that made a difference. Usually it meant being a good husband or wife and a caring parent. It meant doing good to others, preferably quietly, unostentatiously, without expectation of recognition or reward. The people who were most mourned were not the richest, or the most famous, or the most successful. They were people who enhanced the lives of others. They were kind. They were loving. They had a sense of their responsibilities. When they could, they gave to charitable causes. If they could not give money, they gave time. They were loyal friends and committed members of communities. They were people you could count on. Shakespeare's Mark Antony was wrong: the good we do lives after us. For most of us, it is the most important thing that we leave behind.

A tribute at a funeral was invariably more than the story of a life. It was an evocation of a world of values, the values that made families and communities what they were. I learned more from those occasions than I did from many courses of moral philosophy. This was ethics at the cutting edge. A funeral was more than a family burying its dead. It was an affirmation of life and the values that give it purpose and grant us as much of eternity as we will know on earth.

I learned from those occasions that happiness is the ability to look back on a life and say: I lived for certain values. I acted on them and was willing to make sacrifices for them. I was part of a family, embracing it and being embraced by it in return. I was a good neighbour, ready to help when help was needed. I was part of a community, honouring its traditions, participating in its life, sharing its obligations. It is these things that make up happiness in this uncertain world. Taken together, they make us see what is at risk in our present culture.

No one ever asked me to say of someone that they dressed well, lived extravagantly, took fabulous holidays, drove an expensive car or had a good time. I never heard anyone praised for being too busy at work to find time for their children. Our ordinary, instinctive sense of happiness is saner and more humane than the story told by the media and the advertising columns. It

suggests that happiness is not the pursuit of pleasure or the satisfaction of desire. Instead, it is inseparable from living well. It is a
moral concept, and it is made in those places where morality
matters – the family, the congregation, the community – where
we are valued not for what we earn, or what we can buy, or the
way we cast our vote, but simply for what we are and what we do.

16

The third domain

Imagine a town or city exactly like the one in which you live, with one difference. There are no houses of worship. Churches, synagogues, mosques, temples – all vanish overnight. What disappears with them? A great architectural heritage, certainly. Does anything else? I think it does.

For more than a century the social drama of the West has been dominated by politics and economics. There is government on the one hand, the market on the other. One represents the state, the other the individual. The government is us in our collective embodiment. The market is us in our private pursuits, as individuals seeking the satisfaction of our desires. They are about different things. Politics is about the pursuit and distribution of power. Economics is about the pursuit and distribution of wealth. Between them, they have been presumed to hold the solution to most of our social problems.

Neither, though, has been successful in addressing the real problems that have stayed with us and even grown, alongside ever more intricate government intervention and ever more sophisticated and fast-moving markets. I mean the social pathologies of which we are all too well aware – violence, crime, the rise of depressive illness, the breakdown of family relationships, the pervasive sense of loneliness and despair – which brings me back to those overshadowed places in the urban landscape, houses of worship and the communities of faith of which they are the home.

Traditionally, they stood as the matrix of a set of institutions which have grown weaker in recent years: the home, the family, the community, a sense of tradition, the stories through which our ancestors told themselves where they came from and where they were going to, the rituals in which they expressed their togetherness as a congregation in the presence of the Divine, the prayers in which they gave thanks for the world as the gift of God.

They too were about the pursuit and distribution of certain things, but whatever these were, they were not wealth or power. They had a distinctive logic which marked them off from politics on the one hand and economics on the other. The reason is this: wealth and power are – at least in the short run – zero sum games. At any given moment there is only so much of either. If I have total power and then I share it with nine others, I have only a tenth of the power with which I began. Likewise, if I have £1,000 and share it with nine strangers, I am left with only a tenth of what I had. That is why politics and economics are about conflict and competition. They are about the things which, the more I share, the less I possess. The more I give away, the less I have.

Not everything is like that. There are goods which are precisely *not* zero sum games. The more friendship I share, the more I have. The more love I give, the more I possess. The best way to learn something is to teach it to others. The best way to have influence is to share it as widely as possible. These are the things that operate by the logic of multiplication not division, and they are precisely what is created and distributed in communities of faith: friendship, love, learning and moral influence, along with those many other things which only exist by virtue of being shared.

That is why communities of faith heal the wounds opened up by politics and economics. They unite where politics divides.

They foster co-operation where the market focuses on competition. They are the counterweight to the 'war of all against all' that is mediated and institutionalized in the market and the state. They are the third domain: the place where we give expression to the fact that not every relationship is built on power or market exchange. Some at least are built on giving, respect and love. These too, no less than the state and the market, need a home, a place to grow.

17

Faith lost

It was bound to happen, I suppose. We are at the end of one of those long sweeps of the pendulum of history when religion has been on the wane. Matthew Arnold heard it on Dover Beach, the 'melancholy, long, withdrawing roar' of the retreating Sea of Faith. Nietzsche heard it in the words of the madman, rushing to and fro in the market place. 'Whither is God? ... I shall tell you. We have killed him, you and I.' What happened next – two World Wars, the Holocaust, Stalinist Russia – did little to suggest that we were right to have faith in godlessness. Nietzsche was correct in a way he could not have foreseen. The loss of God was, as he sensed, a descent into nightmare and madness. Yet it was understandable.

It came about because, at some time in the sixteenth and seventeenth centuries, people forgot that the task of religion is to bring peace to the world by bringing peace to the soul. Instead, throughout Europe, people fought one another in the name of God. Throughout the Middle Ages there were bloodthirsty clashes between Christianity and Islam. Following the Reformation, war turned inward on Christianity itself. The great wars of religion that scarred the face of Europe led thoughtful people to conclude that there had to be a better way.

If religion were a source of truth, how were we to decide when one religion said one thing and a second another, and each claimed to be the ultimate arbiter? If it were a source of progress, why did it so often act as a roadblock, turning its back on discoveries like those of Galileo? If it were a source of freedom, how did it come to ally itself with monarchs, emperors and the accoutrements of power? Rarely was there a greater gap between the ideal and the real, the map and the territory, what faith taught and what it did.

So people of conscience began to search for another route. Science was born out of the desire to find a path to objective knowledge, a way of testing conflicting claims. Toleration arose out of the conviction that space should exist for rival versions of faith. Freedom came to be seen as an essential part of politics, not least the freedom that comes from giving everyone a share in the governing process, the democratic dream. The irony is that these were all religious ideals which came to be enacted in secular ways because religions lost the script and became diverted from their proper course. They often do.

How does it happen? The great mistakes in human civilization occur when we forget that everything is what it is and not another thing. Religion – the art of bringing heaven down to earth – began to occupy other areas, among them the acquisition of knowledge and the pursuit of power. It dominated the universities. It joined forces with government. It subjected them to a logic that was not theirs. The reaction was inevitable: secularization. First government then the universities declared their independence. The trouble is, having lost faith in religion when it played away, we lost faith in it when it was playing at home.

There is a place for faith at the centre of our lives. The reason is that it speaks to something essential in the human condition. Not everything that matters is fully embraced by the great institutions of modern life: government, the market, science and the leisure and entertainment industry. In a world of ever-accelerating change, we need the rituals and stories that remind us why we are here, that make us feel at home in the world. In an age of massive impersonal forces – the global economy, the earth's environment, international politics, instant worldwide communication – we need an affirmation that we count, individually and irreplaceably. If we are to stay sane, we need something that links us to the totality of what is and gives it a human face through institutions on a human scale.

Without some sense of the transcendent, we lose the script of the human story. We begin to find it hard to say what we are about, what matters and why. The great faiths are our treasury of meanings, and we are meaning-seeking animals. Faith is about the dignity of the personal, and it can never be obsolete.

18

Faith found

Science, politics, economics, anthropology, sociobiology – all answer questions of what and how but not why. The state and the market track change and give it order but not direction. They are neutral on the questions that matter most to us as human beings. What kind of world do we seek to create? Given that we have vast power, how should we use it? We can travel at unprecedented speed, but where do we want to go? The state and the market – our mechanisms for handling power and exchange – are impersonal, neutral, impartial. That is their glory. It is what makes them necessary. At the same time it renders them impotent in dealing with the psychological and social dimensions of change, which are above all personal.

Markets value us for what we can buy. Politicians court us for the way we vote. But to act, create and take risks, we need the self-confidence that comes from being valued for what we are. That was and is the central truth of the great religions, to which all else is commentary. They make a monumental assertion. Each of us is 'the image of God'. We are, as Kant said, ends not just means. We have value in and of ourselves. We exist because of God's love. We survive because of His grace. Though we face the unknown, we are not alone.

These are not abstract truths. The genius of the great faiths was to take these propositions and translate them into lives. They teach us how to build families out of love. How to construct communities out of care. How to say the words and do the deeds that redeem us from our loneliness by creating relationships of trust. Faith brings us back to the why that must precede the how. Why do we work, build, strive? To create a world that gives dignity to the personal, that honours the image of God in the human frame.

This is what sets human history apart from mere evolution. Other animals have survival mechanisms hard-wired into their brains. They are slow to adapt and blind in their adaptation. Natural selection is powerful in the long run but painful in the short. The strong survive and multiply. The weak fail and die. Human existence does not work this way. We are the product not of nature but of culture. We change because we can imagine different worlds and act in accordance with our imagination. We do not act alone. Through the ideals we share and the relationships we make, we are capable of the most formidable collaborative endeavours. We are social animals, the most adaptive the universe has seen. We are also learning animals. We have a sense of destination, therefore we can make continuous adjustments when we drift off course. We can make good our errors – within limits. Understanding our limits is thus essential to hope. We can do godlike things so long as we never mistake ourselves for God.

Communities of faith are where we preserve the values and institutions that protect our humanity, defending it against the constant encroachments of impersonal forces. These are easy to spot. They are the things that turn us into means instead of ends, or substitute prices for values, or see us as products of the system – consumers, voters – rather than as the point of the systems themselves. Impersonal theories erode the meanings that give our lives the dignity of a purpose. They are reductivist: they shrink our stature. They suggest that we are the 'naked ape', the 'selfish gene', a bundle of desires rather than a set of aspirations, the effects of causes rather than living works of art self-created in freedom.

Above all, impersonal theories attack the nervous system of human relationship, that most delicate of connecting tissues. They turn bonds of love into conflicts of power. They substitute exploitation for trust. They reread altruism as self-interest. They develop a 'hermeneutic of suspicion', another name for seeing the worst in everyone and everything, thus learning to distrust the world. They do a search-and-replace operation, reading 'I' in place of 'we'. These manoeuvres are massively dysfunctional. They destroy the cells of togetherness when we most need them, leaving us vulnerable and alone.

It was against just such a scenario that faith was born and will always be reborn. Faith is the ability to move from 'I' to 'Thou'. We are the only beings who are self-conscious. We are thus the only animals that know we are alone. Out of this awareness, our ancestors discovered the astonishing truth that God is found in relationship, communication, in words that bind. Speaking and listening, we can bridge the abyss between my loneliness and yours. That is where faith begins, when we speak to God and hear Him speaking to us, and we know that we are not alone. From that elemental experience is born our ability to form relationships built on trust – on words spoken, words honoured, words that join us to others and others to us. Faith is what redeems us from loneliness and humanizes the world.

19

The art of happiness

There is an art of happiness. It has very little to do with how much money you have, or how much fame, power or success you enjoy. My late father came to Britain at the age of five. He and his family, along with thousands of others like him, were fleeing from persecution in Eastern Europe. At the age of 14 he had to leave school to make a living and support the family. He went into the business my grandfather had started, selling leftovers of cloth in Commercial Road in London's East End.

He did not do very well. I do not think he had a mind for business. I remember days, many of them, when I went to the shop to keep him company and never saw a single customer. Nor did he make friends easily. He was a man of austere moral principles and he could never bear the compromises of everyday life. I do not know how he stayed sane, knowing the chances he might have had in another life, the opportunities that did not come his way, the education he missed. He had a fine mind. He loved music and painting and literature, but he was always conscious that he was self-taught. Yet I never heard him complain. That was the odd thing.

He enjoyed life; and he had faith. I think he enjoyed life because he had faith. He knew certain simple truths and they gave shape to his life. He was a Jew. He was proud of his people and their history. He loved synagogue. He prayed. I do not know how much Hebrew he understood – not much, to be truthful – but those ancient words gave him comfort. In his eighties he underwent four difficult operations. Each time, he would take with him his prayer shawl, phylacteries and prayer book and, most precious of all, a book of Psalms. He would read it and it gave him strength. You could see the change. For him it was like a glass of whisky on a cold day. He never said why or how, but I imagine it was simple enough. God was there, holding him by the hand. Knowing that, he could face whatever fate might bring. When he went into hospital for the fifth operation in his eighty-ninth year, he knew it was the last. He became agitated only once, when he no longer had the strength to pray. 'Pray for me,' were the last words I heard him say.

Even then, though, it was not over. Our son Joshua, his eldest grandchild, had just got engaged. We told him the news. No longer able to speak, he smiled and it was like seeing him as a young man again. The story would continue. He would have great-grandchildren, even if he would not live to see them. The future was going to be OK. He could leave us now. Quietly, without fuss, he did, with my brother Alan at his bedside, reciting the Sabbath morning prayers.

He gave us, his four boys, something precious. Not money or possessions. He never had much of those, nor did they occupy much space in his mind. He gave us ideals. He gave us pride in what we were. He taught us how to love. I took his loss badly. For two years my world fell apart. I could not read, write or concentrate. I felt his absence daily. Then – how it happened, I cannot say; perhaps it was simply an awareness that grew over time – I found comfort. I thought he was not there. Then I realized he was. Something of him lived on in me. I could still see him, hear him, turn to him for advice, knowing what he would say. I could forgive him for some of the things he had said which had hurt and know that he forgave me for the things I had said that had hurt him. I knew that the people who change our lives do not die. They live on in us as we live on in our children. That is as much of immortality as we will ever know this side of the grave, and it is enough.

There is an art of happiness. It has something to do with striving, with ideals, with moral principle; and it has to do with the moments when we relax that striving and take pleasure in what we are and what we have. My late father followed a voice. He heard it and never doubted it and, without saying anything about it, he taught me to recognize it too. Sometimes it is hard to hear, but I have tried to listen to it and follow it wherever it leads. I now know its name. It is called the voice of God.

PART IV

Finding God

20

The face of the personal

There was a moment in Lord Robert Winston's great television series, *The Human Body*, which I can only call a signal of transcendence. Through most of the seven programmes he had spoken as a scientist. He showed us the body in all its wondrous complexity, but it remained just that – a body, a collection of cells genetically programmed to do remarkable things.

Then, at the end of the programme dedicated to the brain, a different Robert Winston spoke. For a few minutes he stood before us wearing a *yarmulka* (the headcovering worn by Jewish men), in a synagogue, reading from a scroll of the Torah. As far as I can recall his words, he said something like this: 'Until now I have spoken as a scientist. That is what I am. That is what I do. And the human brain is something we can study scientifically. But there is something about it that I cannot account for in scientific terms alone – the phenomenon of consciousness. For this I have to reach for a word outside the sphere of science. I call it ... the soul.'

If there is a mystery at the heart of the universe it is here, not in distant galaxies or remote times, but in the human mind. It does not lie in consciousness as such, which we share with other animals, but in self-consciousness, which comes from the unique human gift of language. Because we can speak, we can conceptualize. We can think. We can envisage a world different from the one we currently inhabit. This is an astonishing ability. It means

that we can do more than react to stimuli. We can contemplate
alternatives and choose between them. We can imagine and act
on the basis of our imagination. We have freedom in a way no
other life form has.

For everything else we can give a scientific explanation.
Events are the effects of causes. Determinism reigns. Human
consciousness, however, is not caused by something in the past.
It is oriented towards the future – a future that is radically inde-
terminate because it is made by our choices, which themselves
emerge from the creativity of the mind. As Niels Bohr once said,
if the great scientific discoveries had not been made when and
by whom they were, someone else sometime else would have
discovered them; but if Shakespeare had not written his plays,
they would have been lost for all time. Nothing can predict the
constructs of the human imagination. In freedom of thought
we create new possibilities of action. It is this link between
language, imagination, the ability to contemplate alternative
futures and the freedom to choose between them that frames the
mystery of the human person. It is here also that monotheism –
the single greatest achievement of civilization – found God.

For me faith is the belief in the objective reality of the
personal. The God heard by Abraham, Moses and the prophets
was not a tribal deity, group self-interest projected onto the sky.
Nor was He a member of the pantheon of paganism, a capricious
spirit invoked to explain why things are as they are, a pseudo-
scientific construct rendered redundant by proper science. The
God our ancestors heard was the voice of reality as it responds to
and affirms the personal, echoing our consciousness, telling us
that we are not alone.

There will always be things that science cannot explain –
the beauty of Mozart; the power of a Shakespearean sonnet; the
courage of a Lincoln; the point of a joke; the tenderness of love

between mother and child; the feeling we have when someone recognizes us and smiles. These are worlds brought into being by the freedom of the human spirit. They can never be captured in the language of cause and effect, stimulus and response, blind watchmakers and selfish genes. Nor are these private worlds. We share them, most of the time. Though they arise from and create responses in individual minds, they find expression in public languages, the languages of speech, music, humour, art. Through them our personhood meets other persons and forms relationships of understanding and trust. In the possibility of communication, we discover that we are not alone.

It is here, in the mystery and majesty of the personal, that God lives.

21

The mirror of God

God was always there. Humanity was not. I do not mean in the obvious sense, that there was a time before *homo sapiens* first walked the earth. I mean that the discovery that we are persons with significance and dignity was far from obvious. It was a relatively late achievement in human civilization and surely the most important, for it contained the seeds of much else: the sanctity of life, respect for persons, the free society and recognition of human rights.

For me, the axial moment of civilization came with the words, 'And God created man in His own image; in the image of God He created him; male and female He created them.' Even at this distance of time, it is worth trying to recapture the revolution this sentence set in motion.

The familiar way of writing the history of civilization can be summarized in three sentences. In the beginning people believed in many gods. Monotheism came and reduced them to one. Science came and reduced them to none. Or, in other words, myth was humanity's first attempt at understanding the world. Then came monotheism and stripped the world of myth. Finally, science taught us that we did not even need God. All we needed was observation and the ability to connect one thing to another. God became redundant, or at best the Big Bang. On this view, the Bible was a halfway stage on the long road to science.

That is a view we have come to accept, but it radically misses the point. Here is a quite different way of telling the story. From the dawn of civilization to today, mankind has reflected on its place in the universe. Compared to all there is, each of us is infinitesimally small. We are born, we live, we act, we die. At any given moment our deeds are at best a hand waving in the crowd, a ripple in the ocean, a grain of sand on the human beach. The world preceded us by billions of years, and it will survive equally long after we die. How is our life related to the totality of things? To this, there have always been two answers, fundamentally opposed.

There have been cultures, ancient and modern, that saw the world in terms of vast, impersonal forces. For the ancients these were earthquakes, floods, famines, droughts, together with the processes of nature: birth, growth, decline and death. Today, we are more likely to identify those forces with the global economy, international politics, the environment and the information superhighway. What is common to them all is that they are impersonal. They are indifferent to us, just as a tidal wave is indifferent to what it sweeps away. Global warming does not choose its victims. Economic recession does not stop to ask who suffers. Genetic mutation happens without anyone deciding to whom it will happen.

Seen in this perspective, the forces that govern the world are essentially blind. They are not addressed to us. We may stand in their path, we may step out of the way, but they are unmoved by our existence. They do not relate to us as persons. In such a world, hubris (the idea that we can change things) is punished by nemesis. Human hope is a prelude to tragedy. The best we can aim for is to seize what pleasure comes our way and make ourselves stoically indifferent to our fate. This is a coherent vision, but a bleak one.

At some stage, in ancient Israel, a different vision was born, one that saw in the cosmos the face of the personal: God who brought the universe into being as parents conceive a child, not blindly but in love. We are not insignificant, nor are we alone. We are here because someone willed us into being; someone who wanted us to be, who knows our innermost thoughts, who values us in our uniqueness, whose breath we breathe, and in whose arms we rest; someone in and through whom we are connected to all that is.

That discovery – that we are the image of God, the trace left by Him – was utterly new and explosive in its implications. It meant that the key to interpreting the universe was not force or power but the personal; and the personal is anything but blind. Everything else in the Bible flowed from the attempt to make this fact the foundation of a new social order. The question became: 'What relationships and what kind of society honour the dignity of the person – of all persons in their dependence and independence?' We redeem the world to the degree that we personalize it, taming the great forces so that they serve rather than dominate humanity. That was and remains a marvellous vision. It changed and still changes the world.

In finding God, our ancestors found themselves. Discovering God, singular and alone, they found the human person, singular and alone. Hearing God reaching out to us, they began to understand the significance of human beings reaching out to one another. They began, haltingly at first, to realize that God is not about power but about relationship; that religion is not about control but about freedom; and that God is found less in nature than in society, in the structures we make to honour His presence by honouring His image in other human beings.

This much can never be made redundant by science, for God is dispensable only if humanity is. God is reality with a human face, the mirror without which we cannot see ourselves.

22

The voice of silence

If God exists, Bertrand Russell used to say, then He has written a detective story with all the clues pointing the wrong way.

I understand what he means. Somehow you feel that the biggest thing there is ought to be visible in some way, demonstrable, provable. Why, if God is there, is He so elusive? It is a good question. Even better, because it is so subtle, is the Bible's answer.

The prophet Elijah, one of nature's zealots, has decided to confront the false prophets of Baal. He summons them to Mount Carmel and proposes a simple test. Let us both prepare sacrifices, he says, and call on our deity and see who answers. The God who sends fire is the God who exists.

It is – or so it seems – the perfect test, and one of which the great philosopher would surely have approved. It is a scientific experiment, a controlled trial. It satisfies even the most rigorous demands of logical positivism. Elijah is about to see whether, once and for all, he can prove that God exists.

The event proceeds. The Baal prophets prepare their offering and call on their god. Nothing happens. They intensify their devotions. Still nothing. They begin to work themselves into a frenzy, goring and lacerating themselves. Not a spark. Elijah for once cannot resist a touch of humour. 'Cry louder. Maybe your god is having a sleep.' Eventually they give up, defeated.

Elijah, with the confidence of the true believer, says a few words of prayer, and fire descends. QED. The assembled Israelites, awed and convinced, cry out, 'The Lord is God, the Lord is God.' End of episode – but not quite. The Bible is anything but a simple-minded book.

The trial is the end of Elijah's encounter with the false prophets, but it is not even the beginning of his encounter with God. Unpopular with the powers that be for his treatment of what has become the court religion, a warrant is out for his arrest. He hides. Eventually he finds himself on Mount Horeb, another name for Mount Sinai where, centuries before, the Israelites had received their great revelation of God. There, the following famous scene takes place.

God tells Elijah to stand on the mountain, 'for the Lord is about to pass by'. Suddenly there is a great and powerful wind that tears the mountains apart and shatters the rocks. But God is not in the wind. Then there is an earthquake. But God is not in the earthquake. Then there is a fire. But God is not in the fire. After the fire comes a still, small voice. God is in that voice.

There are many ways of translating the Hebrew phrase for 'a still, small voice'. Some prefer 'a gentle whisper'. Others, more accurate to the original, render it 'the sound of a fine silence'. My own interpretation is different. What is a 'still, small voice'? It is a sound that you can only hear if you are listening.

I suspect that what God was saying to Elijah was this. Your trial was based on error. The prophets of Baal believe that God is power. You showed them that I am a greater power. Perhaps so, but that is not what I am. The idea that God is power is pagan. God does not impose Himself on His image, mankind. On the contrary, God – like a true parent – creates space for His children to grow. He is always there, but only if we seek Him. His word is ever present, but only if we listen. Otherwise we do not hear it at all.

God is the music of all that lives, but there are times when all we hear is noise. The true religious challenge is to ignore the noise and focus on the music. The great command of the Bible, '*Shema Yisrael*', does not mean, 'Hear, O Israel.' It means, 'Listen.' Listening, we hear. Searching, we find.

23

Listening

Sometimes through an encounter with another faith you learn something important about your own. I was much taken by the following story about Mother Teresa of Calcutta.

She was being interviewed by a journalist about her life and faith. At one point the interviewer asked her what she said to God when she prayed.

'I don't say anything,' she replied. 'I just listen.'

'And when you listen,' said the interviewer, 'what does God say?'

'He doesn't say anything,' she replied. 'He just listens.' Before the bewildered journalist could say anything more, she added, 'And if you don't understand that, I can't explain it to you.'

Judaism is a noisy religion. We pray loudly and together. When we sit and study Bible or Talmud, we do so in pairs or groups. We debate, gesticulate, pound the table, as if the fate of the world depended on the outcome of a disagreement between two rabbis from the second or twelfth centuries. We argue with a passion.

I remember my first encounter with the Bet Midrash, the study hall of an Israeli yeshiva. It was one of the great cultural shocks of a lifetime. I had just finished my degree at Cambridge. The university library there was a place of almost sepulchral quiet. A cough could be heard 100 yards away. People sat in the reading room behind piles of books, making notes, studying intently, occasionally leaning back for a moment's reflection, but never saying a word. After that, I could hardly believe what greeted me at the yeshiva – a cacophony of voices in which you could hardly hear yourself speak, let alone think. The vast room was full of tables at which students sat or stood, debating ferociously, reliving ancient 'arguments for the sake of heaven' and sounding as noisy as a football crowd.

Years ago, in the course of a television series on the world's great faiths, the presenter turned his attention to Judaism. Among those he interviewed was the writer Elie Wiesel. 'Professor Wiesel,' he said, obviously taken aback by an encounter not unlike mine, 'Judaism seems to be a very talkative sort of faith. Tell me, are there any silences in Judaism?'

'Judaism is full of silences,' Wiesel replied. Then he paused and added, with a smile, 'But we don't talk about them.'

Faith is about silence, the silence beneath speech. There is a fine passage in the nineteenth Psalm (vv. 1–3):

The heavens declare the glory of God;
The skies proclaim the work of His hands.
Day after day they pour forth speech;
Night after night they communicate knowledge.
There is no speech or language
Where their voice is not heard...

Undergirding all human speech is that sense of 'something far more deeply interfused', as Wordsworth called it, which is the hymn of creation to its creator. Beneath the noise there is the music, but to hear it we need to create a kind of silence of the soul. We need to learn to listen; and listening is an art, one of the greatest there is.

We can define it more precisely. Some 80 years ago the young anthropologist Bronislaw Malinowski, after fieldwork among the Trobriand Islanders of New Guinea, reflected on the role of speech in societies both primitive and modern. He came to a remarkable discovery, one borne out by recent psycholinguistics. Most conversation is not what we assume it to be – the exchange of information. Instead, talk 'serves to establish bonds of personal union between people brought together by the mere need of companionship'. It joins. It creates relationship. It involves an almost tangible sense of the presence of an Other. We call communication 'staying in touch' as if it were a kind of embrace, which it is.

Malinowski called this 'phatic communion', meaning the connection formed when two people talk, regardless of what they say. There is a music beneath the words, and we can say what it is. It is the encounter of two persons in which each recognizes in the other an answering presence. It says that someone else is there, attending to us, listening, responding to our being, confirming our existence. Speech is intimately related to the social, to our need to belong to something larger than the self. Perhaps that is what the noise of the yeshiva was all about. The students were immersing themselves in the words of Torah, the Divine speech heard at Mount Sinai and which, according to Jewish tradition, has echoed ever since.

Prayer is the act of listening to God listening to us. It is phatic communion, the touch of two selves. Yes, there are words, many of them. There is a text, a liturgy, a *siddur*, a proper 'order' of prayer, the libretto constructed by generation after generation of men and women of faith as they searched for the words that would best express their collective thanks to heaven and their hopes for heaven's grace. But there is also a listening beyond words, a silence that gives meaning to speech. In that silence, we know and are known by God.

24

A question of faith

Isidore Rabi, winner of a Nobel Prize in physics, was once asked why he became a scientist. He replied, 'My mother made me a scientist without ever knowing it. Every other child would come back from school and be asked, "What did you learn today?" But my mother used to ask a different question. "Izzy," she always used to say, "did you ask a good question today?" That made the difference. Asking good questions made me a scientist.'

Judaism is a religion of questions. The greatest prophets asked questions of God. The book of Job, the most searching of all explorations of human suffering, is a book of questions asked by man, to which God replies with a string of questions of His own. The earliest sermons usually began with a question asked of the rabbi by a member of the congregation. Most famously, the Seder service on Passover begins with four questions asked by the youngest child.

I can identify with Rabi's childhood memories. When I left university and went to Israel to study in a rabbinical seminary, I was stunned by the sheer intensity with which the students grappled with texts. Once in a while the teacher's face would light up at a comment from the class. '*Du fregst a gutte kashe*,' he would say – 'You raise a good objection.' This was his highest form of praise. Abraham Twerski, an American psychiatrist, tells of how, when he was young, his instructor would relish challenges to his arguments. In his broken English he would say, 'You right! You 100 prozent right! Now I show you where you wrong.'

Religious faith has suffered hugely in the modern world by being cast as naïve, blind, unquestioning. The scientist asks, the believer just believes. Critical inquiry, so the stereotype runs, is what makes the difference between the pursuit of knowledge and the certainties of faith. One who believes in the fundamentals of a creed is derided as a fundamentalist. The word 'fundamentalist' itself comes to mean a simplistic approach to complex issues. Religious belief is too often seen as the suspension of critical intelligence. As Wilson Mizner once put it, 'I respect faith, but doubt is what gets you an education.'

To me, this is a caricature of faith, not faith itself. What is the asking of a question if not itself a profound expression of faith in the intelligibility of the universe and the meaningfulness of human life? To ask is to believe that somewhere there is an answer. The fact that throughout history people have devoted their lives to extending the frontiers of knowledge is a moving demonstration of the restlessness of the human spirit and its constant desire to transcend, to climb. Far from faith excluding questions, questions testify to faith – that the world is not random, the universe is not impervious to our understanding, life is not blind chance.

That, I suspect, is why Judaism encourages questions. On the phrase, 'Let us make man in Our image, according to Our likeness,' Rashi, the eleventh-century biblical commentator, says: 'This means, with the power to understand and to discern.' Critical intelligence is the gift God gave humanity. To use it in the cause of human dignity and insight is one of the great ways of serving God.

It is a point made recently by Timothy Ferris in his survey of contemporary science, *The Whole Shebang* (1997). He suggests that the most reasonable view of the universe, given all we now know, is that if God created it, He did so 'out of an interest in spontaneous creativity'. What would a creative universe look like? It would be one that gave rise to a form of life that was itself creative and unpredictable. That creative lifeform would inquire into the workings of the universe, 'winnowing out the predictable from the unpredictable and inventing theories to account for the difference'. A God who cared for creativity would not provide the answers. He would prefer a universe in which people asked the questions.

I cannot do better than quote Ferris's magnificent closing sentences: 'All who genuinely seek to learn, whether atheist or believer, scientist or mystic, are united in having not a faith but faith itself. Its token is reverence, its habit to respect the eloquence of silence. For God's hand may be a human hand, if you reach out in loving kindness, and God's voice may be your voice, if you but speak the truth.'

Every question asked in reverence is the start of a journey towards God. When faith suppresses questions, it dies. When it accepts superficial answers, it begins to wither. Faith is not opposed to doubt. What it is opposed to is the shallow certainty that what we understand is all there is.

25

Where we let Him in

Rabbi Menahem Mendel of Kotzk (1787–1859) was one of the most remarkable figures of the populist Jewish mystical movement known as Hassidism. Angular, unconventional, passionate in his search for truth, he was compared by the late A. J. Heschel to his Christian near-contemporary, Søren Kierkegaard. Both were complex and tormented figures who spent their lives, like the biblical Jacob, 'wrestling with God and with men'.

It is said that on one occasion, at the third Sabbath meal, when the atmosphere of the holy day is at its most intense, the rabbi turned to his disciples and asked, 'Where does God live?'

They were stunned by the strangeness of the question. 'What does the rabbi mean, "Where does God live?" Where does God not live? Surely we are taught that there is no place devoid of His presence. He fills the heavens and the earth.'

'No,' said the rabbi. 'You have not understood. God lives where we let Him in.'

That story has always seemed to me more profound than many learned volumes of theology. God is there, but only when we search. He teaches, but only when we are ready to learn. He has always spoken, but we have not always listened. The question is never, 'Where is God?' It is always, 'Where are we?' The problem of faith is not God but mankind. The central task of religion is to create an opening in the soul.

The Hebrew Bible goes to inordinate lengths to describe

the construction of the Tabernacle, Israel's first collective 'house of God'. Yet the philosophical problem is glaring. When King Solomon dedicated the Temple in Jerusalem, he said, 'But will God really dwell on earth? The heavens, even the highest heaven, cannot contain You. How much less this house I have built!' The prophet Isaiah said in the name of God, 'The heavens are My throne and the earth is My footstool. Where then is the house you will build for Me? Where will My resting place be?' How can there be a finite home for an infinite God? How can space contain that which is beyond space?

The Hassidic masters supplied the answer. Examining carefully the biblical text, they noted that when God commanded Moses to build the Tabernacle He said, 'I will dwell in them,' not, 'I will dwell in it.' God lives not in the building but the builders; not in holy places but in holy lives and deeds. If we listen, God is closer to us than we are to ourselves. If we do not, He is further away than the most distant star. Religion is an elaborate discipline of paying attention. Faith is the space we create for God.

Faith is not certainty. It is the courage to live with uncertainty. It is not knowing all the answers. It is often the strength to live with the questions. It is not a sense of invulnerability. It is the knowledge that we are utterly vulnerable, but that it is precisely in our vulnerability that we reach out to God, and through this learn to reach out to others, able to understand their fears and doubts. We learn to share, and in sharing discover the road to freedom. It is only because we are not gods that we are able to discover God.

Sadly, religion is often its own worst enemy. There are times, as Feuerbach said, when we make God in our image instead of letting Him remake us in His. We use heaven as the screen on which we project our wishes, dreams, insecurities and fears.

Sometimes we confuse righteousness with its opposite, self-righteousness. The best antidote to this is the Hassidic saying, 'Better the sinner who knows he is a sinner than the saint who believes he is a saint.' God is not the sum of our wants. He is not the answer to our ignorance, the 'God of the gaps', the scientific explanation of the universe. Nor is He the strategic intervener who relieves us from the responsibility of mending the world.

God is the personal dimension of existence, the 'Thou' beneath the 'It', the 'ought' beyond the 'is', the Self that speaks to self in moments of total disclosure when, opening ourselves to the universe, we find God reaching out to us. At that moment we make the life-changing discovery that, although we are utterly insignificant, we are also utterly significant, a fragment of God's presence in the world. We know that eternity preceded us and infinity will come after us, yet we know also that this day, this moment, this place, this circumstance is full of the light of infinite radiance, whose proof is the mere fact that we are here to experience it. At its height, faith is none other than the transfiguring knowledge that, 'Yea, though I walk through the valley of the shadow of death I will fear no evil, for You are with me.'

Knowing, we are known. Feeling, we are felt. Acting, we are acted upon. Living, we are lived. If we make ourselves transparent to existence, then our lives too radiate that Divine presence which, celebrating life, gives life to those whose lives we touch.

PART V

Faith in the Family

26

Faith is a marriage

When Elaine and I were married, I was 22. She was 21. We had no idea what the future would hold. At that time she was practising radiography. For the first few years of our marriage, while I was studying, she was the breadwinner and I the – not very good – housekeeper.

I had gone to university wanting to be an accountant. I then wandered into philosophy. For a while, after graduating, I studied for a doctorate. It did not go well (I eventually completed it 10 years later). I then taught philosophy for two years. I made a foray into law, but soon discovered that it and I did not get on. Then, following an insistent inner voice, I turned to the rabbinate. This involved intensive study and put a huge burden on Elaine. I went into the rabbinate, continuing to teach at our rabbinical seminary. Along the way our three children were born.

Our life together has had its twists and turns. At each stage of the way we were faced with new challenges. Looking back across 29 years of married life, we could not have foreseen the outcome. As I say to people who ask me what it is like being a Chief Rabbi, 'The greatest kindness God ever does for us is that He never lets us know in advance what we're letting ourselves in for.'

We can know the past. We can never know the future. Human life is life lived towards the future, which means facing the unknown. But we faced it together. Without that togetherness, I doubt whether we could have done much of what we eventually did. It is what made our marriage. At difficult times we were there for one another. I do not think it ever occurred to us that we would not be. That is what a marriage is: a journey across an unknown land, with nothing to protect you from the elements except one another. It may not be much, but it is everything. Anyone who has had the privilege of a happy marriage knows that it is the most important and beautiful thing in life. We constantly give thanks that we have had the blessing of bringing three children into the world, loving them and knowing what it means for love to bring new life into existence.

What is a marriage? Words. A commitment. We pledge ourselves to someone else. It is probably the most significant commitment any of us can make, and it depends on our moral determination to honour it. A declaration of marriage does not mean, 'We are man and wife so long as we find each other attractive or compatible; so long as we feel passion for one another; so long as we don't meet someone else more attractive.' It means, 'I will be with you whatever fate brings. I will stay loyal to you. When you need me, I'll be there. When things are tough, I won't walk away.' A marriage can begin in sexual attraction, shared interests or a sense of common destiny, but by moralizing the bond it lifts it to an altogether different plane. A personal commitment is stronger than passion, emotion or attraction. It is a pledge to share a life together, come what may.

Marriage is the paradigm of faith. Western civilization has suffered many false turns through a failure to understand the word *emunah*, the biblical term for faith. Because it entered Europe through Christianity, itself a product of Hellenistic as well as Hebraic culture, faith was assumed to be a form of knowledge. In biblical Hebrew it has no such connotation. *Emunah* means many things – trust, loyalty, fidelity, strength, firmness, affirmation, caring. All these things have to do not with knowledge but with the relationship between persons. They are about willingness to make a binding commitment in the conscious presence of uncertainty.

Emunah means that I take your hand and you take mine and we walk together across the unknown country called the future. It is what I call a covenantal relationship. That is our relationship with God. It is also the relationship of marriage. For the Hebrew Bible, faith is not primarily what Rudolf Otto called it, the *mysterium tremendum*, our sense of nothingness in the face of infinity. It is more human and intimate than that. It is the bond of love in the context of the radical indeterminacy of the future. Faith is what happens when God reaches out His hand to us and we respond in love and trust. It does not mean – any more than a marriage does – that there will be no shocks in store, no crises, no tragedies. It does, however, mean that we will not desert one another. We will have our domestic disagreements, but God will always be there with us. We will always be there with Him.

Faith is the ability to face the future knowing that we are loved and, being loved, find the power to love in return. Faith is a marriage; marriage is an act of faith. It is neither rational nor irrational; rather it is the redemption of loneliness so that we can face the future without fear. Not because we are optimists, nor because we have blind trust, but because we know that someone will be there with us, giving us support, understanding and strength. A slender consolation? Perhaps. But is there any greater? Elaine and I, looking back on those years, know that we could not have done it without one another. So it is between us and God.

27

Love in a loveless world

Some of the best moments in the Hebrew Bible get lost in translation. A particularly important one comes early in the book of Hosea.

God has told the prophet to marry a prostitute. He wants Hosea to know from the inside what it feels like to be God. God too had married a people, joined His fate to theirs and entered a covenant of mutual loyalty. Israel, however, proved faithless. She took other lovers, worshipped strange gods. In a long speech, God tells the prophet how He feels betrayed. Then, abruptly, the tone changes. It is as if, merely by speaking of his first love, God has rekindled it. Although He has been abandoned, He cannot abandon. He will bring Israel back to the places they once visited, the desert where they first pledged their love. They will renew their marriage. Then comes the sentence with which translators have wrestled. 'In that day – declares the Lord – you will call Me "my husband"; you will no longer call Me "my master".'

The reason the verse is hard to translate is that it involves a complex pun. The key words in Hebrew are *Ish* and *Baal*, and they both mean 'husband'. Hosea is telling us about two kinds of marital relationship – perhaps even two kinds of culture. One is signalled by the word *Baal*, which not only means 'husband' but is also the name of the Canaanite god. Baal, one of the central figures in the pantheon of the ancient Near East, was the storm god of lightning and the fertility god who sends rain to impregnate the ground. He was the macho deity who represented sex and power on a cosmic scale.

Hosea, punning on the name, hints at the kind of world that happens when you worship sex and power. It is a world without loyalties. It is one where relationships are casual, where people are taken advantage of and then dropped. A marriage predicated on the word *Baal* is a relationship of male dominance in which women are used not loved, owned not respected. The word *Baal* means, among other things, 'owner'.

Against this Hosea describes a different kind of relationship. Here his literary device is not pun but quotation. In using the word *Ish* to describe the relationship between God and His people, the prophet is evoking a verse at the beginning of Genesis – the words of the first man seeing the first woman: 'This is now bone of my bones and flesh of my flesh. She shall be called "woman" [*ishah*] for she was taken out of man [*ish*].' Daringly, Hosea suggests that the making of woman from man mirrors the creation of humanity from God. First they are separated, then they are joined again, but now as two distinct persons, each of whom respects the integrity of the other. What joins them is a new kind of relationship built on fidelity and trust.

Despite the distance of almost 3,000 years, Hosea's question is ours. Can there be, in a world driven by sex and power, genuine relationship? Can two persons come together not for mutual exploitation but in love and loyalty – in love that is loyalty – each respecting the dignity of the other and yet working together to do what neither can achieve alone, above all to bring new life into the world? Hosea's originality is to see that the relationship between God and mankind is the relationship between husband and wife. How we see faith determines how we understand marriage.

The world of ancient myth is one in which the strong win, relationships are built on power and whose ultimate price is loneliness. Hosea sees the possibility of another kind of world, built not on dominance but on faithfulness and love. That is what makes him so contemporary a voice. The world he sought is the one we are in danger of losing. The loss of marriage as the ultimate personal commitment is more than a mere shift in social structures. It is the prelude to a less human world – a world of power without morality, sex without love, childhood without stability and relationships without trust.

28

Fractured families

It took a long time for us to realize that by cutting down rain forests, using cars with highly leaded fuels and building factories with toxic emissions we were gradually destroying the ecosystem within which we live and breathe. We know now. It has been much harder for us to realize that by destabilizing marriage and accepting casual sex, serial relationships, divorce and single parenthood as norms we are rapidly eroding the social structures on which humanity depends, but it is no less true.

Families matter in all sorts of ways. Children are among the most vulnerable members of society. How we treat them is one of the best measures of the kind of people we are. Children have fared badly in our affluent world. They have less of their parents' time and attention, less security at home, than a generation or two ago. A mountain of research has counted the cost. Children today are more prone to depression, anxiety, suicidal feelings, drug and alcohol abuse, violence and crime than at any point in recent times. What kind of adult world is it that indulges itself and neglects its children?

No less scandalous are the myths we have invented to justify all this: that 'quality time' makes up for lack of time; that child-care is the same as parental care; that what we cannot give, we can pay others to give; that all sorts of families – dual parent or single parent, stable or fractured, lasting or temporary, male-female or single sex – are the same in their effects upon a child.

No future generation will understand how we convinced ourselves that we really believed these things.

Particularly tragic is the loss of fatherhood. Today in Britain and America almost 40 per cent of children grow up in homes in which their father does not live, and by the time they reach 18 this figure will have risen to one in two. Children who grow up with only one of their biological parents – almost invariably the mother – are disadvantaged in many ways. They are more likely to do badly at school, leave school early, become unemployed, and fail to make successful marriages. Fatherlessness is a major new source of poverty, only marginally remedied by government attempts to ensure payment of child support.

As Margaret Mead has pointed out, the critical test of any civilization is how it socializes males. There is a fundamental difference between motherhood and fatherhood. Motherhood is a biological phenomenon. Virtually without exception in human societies and in most of the animal kingdom, mothers develop a close bond with their children through pregnancy and nurturing. Fatherhood, by contrast, is a social construct. Biologically, the contribution of the father ends with impregnation. In many animal species, fathers do not recognize their children after a few months. What makes human beings different is their uniquely high paternal investment. This is necessary because of the long dependency period of human childhood, itself due to the size of the human brain and the need for children to be born before physical development is complete. Only societies that can enlist the energies of men as partners in the long parenting process can flourish for any length of time.

Human parenthood is a massive commitment, and one to which we are not genetically predisposed. Left without rules, males prefer promiscuity as a means of distributing their genes into the future. That is why marriage and its attendant sanctions

– the sacredness of the marriage ceremony, social disapproval of infidelity – are crucial to its success. In return, the societal gain is vast. It means that adult males share in the work of raising the next generation. They invest income into the family. They enforce discipline, especially in the case of teenage sons. They have an educational role. The word for 'male' in Hebrew comes from the same root as 'memory', reminding us that fathers are often key vehicles of cultural transmission. Together, fathers and mothers enable their children to understand the difference between the sexes, their distinctive cognitive and affective styles, and thus develop emotional intelligence.

Being a social construct, fatherhood is vulnerable in a way motherhood is not. I sometimes wonder whether God is portrayed as a father in the Hebrew Bible not because ancient Israel was a patriarchal society – it was, in aspiration, an egalitarian one – but precisely to invest fatherhood with dignity and sanctity.

My guess is that in the end we will have to turn to our faith traditions to remind us of what we know, but which so much of contemporary culture persuades us to forget. Families are the crucible of our humanity. They are the miniature world in which we learn how to face the wider world. Strong families beget strong individuals, people able to confront the future without fear. Fractured or unstable families beget individuals not fully at home in the world. They grow up angry or anxious, aggressive or defensive, not at peace with others or themselves. For good or bad, the family is the seedbed of the future. Stability and love are its sun and rain. It is the best way we have yet found of replacing insecurity with trust and making love the generative principle of life.

29

C

John Diamond is a brilliant journalist. He is also suffering from cancer. It was diagnosed in March 1997, just a few days after he and his wife Nigella had been to us for dinner. It has been painful to watch him wrestle with the angel of death, but it has also been – the word is unavoidable – inspiring, because John, with immense courage, decided not to keep his condition private but to write about it in his newspaper columns.

He has been given strength by the many thousands of people who have written to him, wishing him well, praying for him, telling him how much his writing means to them. He has also given strength to thousands of other sufferers who, until now, had often not been able to talk about their condition because it was one of those things you did not mention. Talking is part of healing, not because it cures physical illness, but because it gives us the strength that comes from knowing we are not alone. Pain shared is pain halved, or, more precisely, pain with some of the anxiety removed. When it comes to fear, what we can name we can tame.

John also wrote a book about his illness, called *C*, subtitled 'Because Cowards Get Cancer Too'. It is witty, wise and very moving. Towards the end there is a passage that shines with truth. It is night and he is sitting with Nigella in bed:

'What are you smiling at?' she said.

I didn't realise that I was, but what I was thinking about was Nigella and the children...

'It's such a strange time, isn't it?' I said.

'How so strange?'

'Oh you know. Strange in that I've never felt more love for you than I have in the past year, that I've never appreciated you as much, nor the children. In a way I feel guilty that it should have taken this to do it, I suppose. But it is strange, isn't it?'

For the first time, I found myself talking like this without resenting that it had taken the cancer to teach me the basics, without resenting that there was part of me capable of talking like a 50s women's magazine article without blushing.

I still don't believe that there is any sense in which the cancer has been a good thing but, well, it is strange, isn't it?

It is, but I know what he means. The prospect of death is a blowtorch that burns away the irrelevancies and lets us face what really matters. What matters to most of us is what matters to John: marriage, children, home, friends, the support they give when we really need it, the sense we have of being part of a fabric woven from other lives as well as our own, that we are intimately connected to other people, that we have left our trace on them and they on us, that we are not particles free-floating in space but part of an intricate web of relationships joined in companionship and love. How tragic that it has become so hard to say these things and that it sometimes takes tragedy to remind us of them.

Marriage is one of the most majestic achievements of civilization, bringing together in a single institution the great biological forces, ethical imperatives, social needs and emotional investments. It takes sex, love, companionship, economic partnership, procreation, the nurturing of children and their socialization, and out of these things it fashions a work of living art. Tolstoy was wrong when he said all happy marriages are the same. Each is different, a world in its own, and to have been part of the making of one is one of the greatest sources of fulfilment there can be. Often it is the difficult moments that make a marriage mature. As long as Adam and his wife were living in the Garden of Eden he called her 'woman' and blamed her for their sin. Only as they left Eden to face hardship together did he name her Eve, meaning 'the source of life'. Far from being grounds for divorce, it is the crises that bring us together, showing us how, by sharing our vulnerabilities, we can discover strength.

Happiness is as strong as the bonds between us, and no bonds are deeper than those of marriage and parenthood. When a culture forgets this, it is losing the script of the human story.

30

Learning to love

We laugh at the things that give us pain. It is no accident, therefore, that the primal Jewish story is about the family.

Three elderly Jewish ladies are sitting on the beach in Miami, talking about – what else? – their children.

'My son,' says one, 'is such a wonderful son. Every month he sends me $500.'

'You think that's special?' says the second. 'Every month my son sends me $1,000.'

'Feh!' says the third. 'That's nothing. My son spends $500 a *week* on his psychiatrist. And who do you think he talks to him about? Me. Only me.'

Families are not easy places. They are full of stress. They always were. Genesis, the opening book of the Bible, is a set of variations on the theme of family, and none runs smoothly. With Adam and Eve comes conflict. With Cain and Abel, fratricide. Abraham and Sarah disagree about Ishmael. Isaac and Rebecca face the sibling rivalry of Esau and Jacob. Jacob has to contend with the jealousy between his sons. Over them all hovers the figure of God, author of life, and at times we can almost imagine Him saying, 'You think you have problems with your children. What about Me?'

Yet the Hebrew Bible, and Judaism subsequently, never lost sight of the fact that the family is the DNA out of which we build a humane world. There could be no greater contrast than that between the Bible and the world of myth. The ancient epics are about gods and demi-gods whose battles shape the world. They are about cosmic forces and mythic heroes. With Genesis, for the first time in human history, we meet ordinary people living ordinary lives, trying to do their best in a difficult world. That is the great power of the book of books and the reason why it has never lost its hold on the human imagination. It is about us, people we can recognize and identify with. The Hebrew Bible is the ultimate democratic text, because it tells us that each of us matters. We are each the 'image of God'. The real dramas are not the ones fought in court or on the battlefield, by military heroes and kings. Nor are they the ones we read about in the press or see on the television news. They are the ones fought and resolved in the home, between parents and children, husbands and wives. No literature more systematically expresses the dignity of the personal, the high moral drama of everyday life.

The family is where the world acquires a human face, where vast metaphysical themes take on the recognizable contours of people we know. I am born into a world that has already existed for billions of years. I will die knowing that it will continue without me. I exist without having willed myself into being. These facts mock our modern conceit that choice is all and that I am precisely what I will myself to be. Without some human connection to the world-that-is-not-me, however, I become a random accident of evolution, the latest product of the selfish gene, chemical dust on the surface of eternity.

Through my parents I have a history. Through my children I have posterity. In the family I learn the complex choreography of love – what it means to give and take and share, to grow from obedience to responsibility, to learn, challenge, rebel, make mistakes, to forgive and be forgiven, to argue and make up, to win without triumph and know when to lose graciously. It is where we acquire emotional intelligence, that delicate negotiation between the given and the chosen, the things I will and the things resistant to my will.

G. K. Chesterton was right when he said, 'The family is a good institution because it is uncongenial … Aunt Elizabeth is unreasonable, like mankind. Papa is excitable like mankind. Our youngest brother is mischievous, like mankind.' James Q. Wilson put it more eloquently: 'We learn to cope with the people of this world because we learn to cope with the members of our family. Those who flee the family flee the world; bereft of the former's affection, tutelage, and challenges, they are unprepared for the latter's tests, judgements and demands.'

Families are not ideal worlds. They are significant precisely because they are real worlds with people we know and trust. Working out our tensions with them, we learn how to resolve our tensions with society. They are where we count, where we make a difference, where we first find that others are there for us and we must be there for them. And, yes, they have their share of pain. It is the pain of life lived in relationship. Without it we could not learn to love.

31

Being a parent

As a theme in the Bible, it is hard to miss. The first command Adam and Eve are given is to 'be fruitful and multiply'. In short, 'Become parents.' For the first time, biological necessity is elevated to the status of a religious deed.

In only one place in the Bible are we told why God made a covenant with Abraham. 'I have chosen him so that he may instruct his children and his household after him to keep the way of the Lord by doing what is right and just.' Abraham is singled out, not because of his own righteousness, but to be a parent, handing his values on to his children.

When, at the end of his life, Moses comes to sum up his teachings in what to Jews are the most famous lines of the Bible, he says, 'Hear, O Israel … These commandments that I give you today are to be upon your hearts. Teach them repeatedly to your children, speaking about them when you sit at home or walk on the way, when you lie down and when you rise up.' Faith is a conversation between the generations.

Why? The great eleventh-century poet and philosopher Judah Halevi spelled out an essential difference between the God of the philosophers and the God of Abraham. For the philosophers, God was an 'It'. For the prophets, He was a 'Thou'. In philosophy, God is a concept, the cause of causes, a logical construct, but in Judaism, God is a person, someone to whom we can speak and who speaks to us.

Today, science has returned to questions about the birth of the universe. Stephen Hawking, in a famous phrase, wrote that if we could understand the origins of matter we would 'know the mind of God'.

From the perspective of faith, however, this is fundamentally to miss the point. What is religiously significant is not the *how* of creation but the *why* – and it was here that Judaism uttered its revolutionary proposition. God did not create the world as a scientist in a laboratory. He brought it into being as parents give birth to a child: not out of curiosity, but in love. We are not the accidental outcomes of a blind evolutionary process. We are the children of the living God.

The prophets used many metaphors for our relationship with God. They called him king, ruler, creator, master, man of war, shepherd of the flock, a potter making man from clay; but the image to which they constantly returned was that of a parent. God is 'our Father'. Isaiah even describes God as a mother. 'Can a woman forget her baby or disown the child of her womb? Though she might forget, I will not forget you.' There is no mistaking God's cry when His people are enslaved. It is the voice of an anguished parent: 'My child, my firstborn, Israel.'

Our most profound religious knowledge comes not from science but from the experience of being a parent. As one new parent put it, 'Since having a child I can relate better to God. Now I know what it feels like to create something you can't control!' Conversely, our most intimate sense of connection with God comes from reflection on what it is to be a child. If we are ever to find peace of mind, however long it takes, we have to make our peace with our parents; and however long it takes, we have to make our peace with God.

Faith is rehearsed and becomes real in the family. Without it, we would not know what its most basic concepts mean.

Through love as the bond between parents and children we understand the love of God for mankind. Through the trust that grows in families, we discover what it is to have trust in God and His world.

32

What we give our children

Fathers, according to a survey by the Rowntree Foundation, are confused about their role. They find themselves caught between the twin demands of 'providing' and 'being involved', being a breadwinner and a carer. They want to do both – to give their children money and time – but it is getting harder, especially in a consumer culture. As one 16-year-old girl put it, 'I think the biggest strain I am on my dad is that I'm constantly bugging him for money.' It is a real dilemma. Is there an answer?

Within days of the report's publication, I found myself at a very emotional public event. It was the sixtieth anniversary of Kindertransport, the operation to rescue thousands of Jewish children from Germany and Austria where they faced almost certain death. More than 1,000 of those who made the journey had come together from across the world to remember. They recalled those fearful days when they waved goodbye to their parents, often never to see them again, and travelled to safety in a strange land.

The most moving speech that day came from the film producer Lord Attenborough. In 1939 he and his family were living in Leicester. His parents had offered refuge to a number of Jewish children escaping from Germany, on their way to the United States. When war was declared, two Jewish girls were staying with them. They realized that they would now be unable to cross the Atlantic. What was to be done?

The Attenboroughs decided that they would offer the girls a home for the duration of the war, but they felt that it was a decision that could only be made as a family. Richard described how his parents called him and his two brothers into the study and told them the situation. They explained that the two girls, Helga and Irene, were Jewish. Their parents had been sent to concentration camps and were unlikely to survive. The girls had no one to care for them and nowhere to go.

Sixty years on, Lord Attenborough recalled his parents' words. 'We want to adopt the girls. We think it is the right thing to do. But we will only do it if you agree. It will call for sacrifices. We were a family of five. Now we will be a family of seven. There will be things we won't be able to afford. There will be things you'll have to share. One of those will be love. You know how much we love you. But now you will have to share that love with Helga and Irene. We will have to show them special affection, because you have a family, but now they have no one at all.'

The boys agreed. Thinking back to that day across six decades, Lord Attenborough described it as the most important day of his life. We in the audience knew what he meant. He had been invited by his parents to join them in an act of courage and generosity. He had been given the chance to sacrifice something for someone else. Was this, I wondered, where he first acquired that moral passion so evident in his subsequent career, in films like *Gandhi* and *Cry Freedom*?

Not all of us face tests like these, but they tell us something important. It is not the things we buy our children that shape their lives, it is the values we give them and the way we invite them to be our partners in building a better world. Wordsworth put it best:

> *What we have loved*
> *Others will love, and we will teach them how.*

PART VI

The Moral Voice

33

Our creation

Media-watchers measure the importance of news stories in terms of column inches. By that standard the Bible has a very strange set of priorities indeed. The creation of the universe, from distant galaxies to insects, takes a mere 34 verses – the first chapter of Genesis and the beginning of the second. By contrast, the creation of the sanctuary, the portable place of worship made by the Israelites in the desert, takes between 500 and 600 verses. It is a bewildering disparity. It is not as if the sanctuary had lasting significance in the history of Israel or mankind: it was a fragile affair, made of beams, hangings and movable objects, and was eventually replaced by the Temple in Jerusalem and then, when that was twice destroyed, by the synagogue. What is this coded message about the relative weight of what matters?

We have, I think, paid a heavy price for seeing the Hebrew Bible as a book of information, a set of facts, a kind of *History of the World, Part One*, or, better yet, an early scientific treatise on the origins of matter, the *Good Book of the Big Bang*. By those standards we can do better now than our ancestors, whose knowledge of such matters came from tales told around the camp fire and strange messages from ecstatic prophets. Jewish tradition gave the Bible, in particular the Mosaic books, a quite different name and one, surely, much closer to its point. They called it *Torah*, meaning 'teaching', 'instruction', and even 'law', always provided that we understand the word 'law' in its widest sense to include ethical principles, moral codes and exemplary lives.

The Hebrew Bible is the answer to a question – not 'What happened?' but 'How then shall we live?' It is, I believe, the most honest, searching, compelling account of what it is to construct a human society on the principles of freedom, justice and compassion, recognizing in every human life the image of God. Yes, I know and feel the many moral difficulties within the book itself, but it is a story, a narrative, an account of things that took time. In this itself it moves to a greater level of sophistication than any philosophical text. Philosophy, that 'series of footnotes to Plato', constructs its system in a timeless zone, whereas the Hebrew Bible recognizes that moral achievement takes time and is the work of many generations. Ideals do not materialize at once. The human story is a tale of many false turns and digressions, but there is a destination, and as long as we do not lose sight of it, we are not without hope.

This is, ultimately, why the Hebrew Bible spends so much more time talking about humanity than about God. It is easy for an infinite creator to make a home for humanity. It is hard for us to make a home for God. That is why making the sanctuary takes up so much more space in the narrative than the birth of the universe. We are interested in God's creation, but God is also interested in our creation – the world we make that honours Him by honouring the trace of His presence in other people.

The name of God's creation is nature. The name of our creation is society. Each is constructed according to laws, but they are different kinds of law. Laws of nature are those that describe. They chart relationships of cause and effect. The world they describe is determined. It does not know freedom other than as chaos. Laws of society are the opposite. They prescribe rather than describe. They are about choices between futures, not about causes that lie in the past. They are precisely about freedom and order – about how to construct a human freedom that respects order, and a human order that honours freedom.

In relation to nature, God is creator, but in relation to society, God is a teacher. Having created the natural world, He asks us to create the social world. He gives us guidance, encouragement, and most of all His faith in us that we can do it. Beyond that, however, He leaves us free – to build or destroy, to hurt or heal. The moral enterprise is the greatest religious drama known to mankind. It is our creation, under the tutelage of God.

34

The moral maze

Most people I meet are moral. They want to be good people. They want to do the right thing. They care about being decent parents and neighbours and citizens. If you are in trouble, they will help. If you need a listening ear, they are there. Why, then, are we so confused about morality? Why do we almost seem to take it for granted that values are relative, that judgement is wrong, that morality is a private affair?

One reason is that not all cultures are identical. I remember one occasion when I had been awarded an international prize for my work in Jewish education. After the award ceremony in Jerusalem, a reception was held in our honour at the home of a leading figure in Israeli life. He made a speech. Luckily it was in Hebrew, so that not everyone there understood what he was saying. In it he delivered a splendid put-down: 'I see that the Chief Rabbi has been given a prize for his contribution to religious education. Well, religious education is better than nothing, but…' He then proceeded to deliver a diatribe against religious schools and argued that what we really needed were secular institutions.

It was probably not the best moment to say so. A few days later, back in London, I told the story to the Israeli ambassador and concluded, 'Now I understand why, after 4,000 years, the Hebrew language still does not contain a word that means "tact"!' Some cultures value understatement and the 'I couldn't possibly comment on that' Sir Humphrey school of diplomacy. Others prefer to tell it as it is.

Then there is the hairdresser I go to in Jerusalem. I do not go there often, so he always forgets who I am. 'Where are you from?' he always asks in Hebrew.

'England,' I reply.

'Ah,' he says with a scowl, 'I fought against the English in 1947.' And then his face creases into a smile. '*Aval ha-anglim hem gentelmanim*' – 'But the English are gentlemen.' Even to say the word, he has to use English. There are English virtues, French virtues, Jewish, Christian and Islamic virtues. Each enriches the world. The fact that cultures are different, however, does not mean that values are relative, any more than the fact that languages are different means that all statements are relative.

Then again, our culture has developed a fascination for moral dilemmas that have no easy answer – abortion, for example, or voluntary euthanasia. We hear them debated, often with equal passion and cogency on both sides, and conclude that morality is a matter of choice. We forget that what makes these dilemmas interesting is that they are exceptions, not the rule. They are conflicts of right and right, not right and wrong. What is more, we tend nowadays to frame them in a way that makes them insoluble, by using the word 'rights' – in the case of abortion, for example, by setting the foetus' right to life against the woman's right to choose. Rights are the worst way to think through dilemmas, because they make absolute claims, allowing no room for compromise. Abortion becomes much easier to think about when we speak of duties – our duties to the mother and the unborn child. We are used to resolving conflicts of duty. They are not easy, but neither are they insoluble. The existence of dilemmas no more disproves objective moral standards than the fact that some things are grey disproves the existence of black and white.

Moral issues are rarely simple, but they are certainly not, except in very rare cases, relative or subjective. The mantras of our culture – 'Do your own thing', 'Whatever works for you', 'Morality is what you feel good after' – are nonsense, and we know it. We know that not every way of life is equally good, or wise, or right. We know that violence and dishonesty and hypocrisy are wrong. We know there is a difference between being a good parent and one who is not there when their children need them. We know that friendship requires certain virtues – trust, confidentiality, loyalty, respect. We know that certain courses of action – a life on drugs, a lack of self-control, an inability to delay the gratification of desire – will end in misery. We know these things as surely as we know anything.

So ignore the experts. Listen instead to the voice of intuition and the memory banks of our great moral traditions. We live at one of those moments when our consciences are wiser than our culture.

35

Values we share

Despite cultural differences, moralities are variations on a theme, the theme of how to live together graciously, preserve the world for the sake of future generations, and create a maximal balance between order and freedom. There are five basic problems any society has to confront if it is to endure, and they give rise to five sets of virtues.

The first is best explained by the question, 'What do porcupines do in winter?' If they stay too far apart, they freeze. If they get too close, they hurt each other. The problem is how to stay close enough for warmth while allowing enough space for comfort. The Bible translates this simply into human terms. On the one hand, each of us is 'the image of God'. On the other hand, 'It is not good for man to be alone.' We are dignified but vulnerable. We need the space to be independent, but we also need relationships that allow us to be interdependent. How do we preserve individual freedom while at the same time sustaining togetherness? The solution lies in the great covenantal virtues – love, compassion, fidelity, integrity, honesty and trust – which bind us together in relationships of mutual support without power or exploitation.

The second has to do with the fact that worthwhile achievement takes effort and time. Knowledge involves study, skills need apprenticeship, and accomplishment is never immediate. We need strength to last the course. Civilization is built on our ability to delay instinctual gratification. From this arise the classic virtues of persistence, self-control, industry and moderation – the things that give us the stamina to learn, grow and create.

The third emerges from the inevitability of conflict. We are beings with open-ended desires, but we are set in a world of finite resources. This means that the human situation is an arena of competing interests and wills. After long and bitter experience, most societies arrive at the conclusion that the rule of law is preferable, by way of conflict resolution, to the rule of power and force. This gives rise to the great procedural virtues of politics – justice, fairness, equity and impartiality.

The fourth has to do with time. It arises from the fact that we are born into a world that long preceded us and will continue to exist when we are no longer here. That imposes obligations on us to both the past and the future. A Talmudic story puts it nicely. A certain rabbi passed a man planting a carob tree. 'How long,' he asked, 'will it take for the tree to bear fruit?'

'Seventy years,' the man replied.

'Are you so sure,' asked the rabbi, 'that you will be here in 70 years' time?'

'No,' replied the man, 'but just as I found carob trees in the world, planted by my grandparents, so I am planting this for my grandchildren.'

We are guardians of the past for the sake of the future. That is what led Edmund Burke to call society a contract between the living, the dead and those not yet born. So we have a responsibility to conserve our natural and human environment, and this calls for virtues such as piety, awe, reverence, respect for life beyond human life, and a responsible stance towards the integrity of nature and culture.

The fifth and final feature has proved to be the most difficult, but without it we fail. How do we deal with outsiders – who have historically included foreigners, minorities, slaves, women and people of a different colour, race or creed? The history of humanity in response to this question has been far from encouraging. It tells a story of intolerance, hatred, persecution, exploitation, ethnic cleansing and attempted genocide. It has proved relatively easy to love our neighbour, but exceptionally hard to love the stranger. Nonetheless, this too is necessary if we are to live together as brothers and sisters under the parenthood of God.

Western civilization has suggested two approaches. The first was the way of Immanuel Kant, who argued that reason has the power to make us see that human duties are universal. The second was the route taken by David Hume, who suggested that it is not reason but emotion – empathy, sympathy, feeling with and for others – that leads us to recognize the humanity of our fellow human beings.

The Hebrew Bible takes a third approach, in some ways more powerful than the others. It speaks not of reason or emotion, but of memory: 'Do not oppress the stranger, for you understand the heart of the stranger. You were once strangers in the land of Egypt.' When we remember the suffering we or our ancestors experienced, we learn not to inflict it on others. What we forget, we can repeat; what we remember serves as the voice that says, 'Never again.' Memory, suggests the Bible, is the moral tutor of mankind.

Whichever way we arrive at the conclusion, though, it amounts to the declaration that one who is not in our image is nonetheless in God's image. This gives rise to the liberal virtues of tolerance, civility and respect for differences, and without them no society can be open, diverse or free.

These features, then, form the shared language of morality. They arise from the human situation as such, and from our five needs: for association, persistence, the peaceful resolution of conflict, handing on to the future what the past has handed on to us, and the space to be different and yet included. Without them no society can long survive, for it will fail to honour the human spirit, against which no force can prevail indefinitely.

36

Can we make moral judgements?

David Selbourne has got it right. In a recent pamphlet, *Moral Evasion*, he lists the 11 arguments now regularly deployed to sabotage any attempt to make moral judgements. They are:

- There is nothing you can do about it.
- It has never been any different.
- There is no quick fix.
- It is the price of a free society.
- You must move with the tide.
- You cannot turn back the clock.
- The problem is much more complex than you think.
- It is beyond the reach of the law.
- You are focusing on the wrong issue.
- Who are you to talk?
- Everyone is doing it, so how can you object?

The result is one of the strangest cultural moments in history. What other ages found offensive – crudity, incivility, obscenity, blasphemy – are today so commonplace as to be routine. Meanwhile, what other generations saw as essential to civilization – moral judgement, the capacity to discriminate between right and wrong – have become not just controversial but taboo. Merely to suggest that there may be some ways of life more gracious, honourable, decent, benign or just plain good than others is to risk accusations of judgementalism and moral panic. Hell hath no fury like a relativist scorned.

It is therefore worth reminding ourselves why every other age apart from ours has cherished moral wisdom. It is not because people wished to interfere in what others did in private. That may sometimes have happened, but it is not what morality is about. It is because life is short and the bill for our mistakes is long. A child may bear the scars of a broken family for a lifetime. Trust, once broken, is hard to repair. An impulsive word can destroy a friendship. A single act of folly may wreck a career. Not everything we want to do is something we ought to do. Our own happiness – let alone civilization itself – depends on our ability to hold desire in check, restrained by thoughts of long-term consequences and consideration for other people. That is where the moral sense is born.

It does not come naturally. Morality is not genetically coded. It is not hard-wired into our brains. That is what gives us our unique evolutionary advantage. *Homo sapiens* is the animal that learns. Moreover, we learn cumulatively, by not having to start afresh in each generation. Instead, through families and schools, we pass on the wisdom of the past, experience often bought at a high price.

What makes humanity different from other life forms is our ability to think beyond the present. We remember what worked and what failed. We are capable of envisaging a different and better world. We can tell the difference between what is and what ought to be. We also know that, whatever world we seek, we cannot make it alone. Therefore we need to create a shared language of the imagination together with relationships of trust. At most times, therefore, most societies have invested vast energies in the institutions through which children learn how best to behave – families, schools, public codes of behaviour, together with the stories, songs and canonical texts through which a culture conveys its memories and ideals.

Reducing morality to private choice is as absurd as the idea that we can each invent our own treatments to cure disease and that the existence of doctors is a threat to our autonomy. Ignore the critics. David Selbourne is right. Moral wisdom is never certain or complete, any more than medicine is certain or complete, but it is something we inherit and learn and share. Above all, it is something we are right to teach our children.

37

The hardest word to hear

For 50 years Goldberg had been the most regular of synagogue attenders. Twice a day he was there to say his prayers. Then suddenly he was not there. Weeks passed and his familiar face was missing.

One day the rabbi met him and asked him what was wrong. Goldberg immediately came to the point. 'For 50 years, rabbi, I have come to the synagogue. Then for the first time I asked for something. I prayed to win the National Lottery. I kept praying and I didn't win. So why should I come any more? God didn't answer my prayer.'

'You are mistaken,' said the rabbi. 'God did answer your prayer. It's just that the answer was "No".'

I like that story because, in its gentle way, it reminds us of a difficult truth. The hardest word to hear in any language is the one that means 'No'.

I know many good and thoughtful people who find it difficult to understand why Judaism – or, for that matter, all the great religions of revelation – contain so many 'thou shalt not's. Does God really mind what we eat, or who we marry, or what we do on the seventh day? Surely faith – they say – is about the big, positive, spiritual things: love, compassion, justice and peace. Can we really experience the Divine in the small print of biblical law, the dense thickets of prohibition? Surely these are the work of men, anxious to build walls around the citadel of faith. God is too vast to be concerned about the minutiae of human behaviour. God is in the great 'Yes', not the small-minded 'No'.

I have much sympathy for this line of thought, but I wonder whether it can really be so. Every affirmation is also a denial. Every commitment is also a gesture of self-restraint. Without the strength to say 'No', we lack the ability to say 'Yes'. When two people pledge themselves to one another in marriage, they are saying 'No' to adultery. When two friends speak in confidence, they are tacitly agreeing not to share their remarks with others. Without restraint there can be no trust. Our 'Yes' implies a 'No'.

Something of the kind applies to every serious achievement. Unless we can say 'No' to distractions, we will never finish the book, or run the marathon, or fix the leaking tap, or take the time we promised to spend with our children. Something always crops up to turn our mind to other things.

One of the siren calls of our culture is 'having it all'. Behind it lies the idea that we can do, or be, or have everything – if not all at once, then at least serially. There are no hard choices, no irreconcilable conflicts, no genuine dilemmas. There is no 'Yes' to something that entails a definite 'No' to something else.

This is the ethics of fantasy. Fortunately, the real world regularly reminds us that there are things that need genuine commitment, even courage. To be a faithful marriage partner, a good parent, a true friend, a decent employer or employee, involves the kind of loyalty that says 'No' to a hundred temptations. Out of such 'No'-saying, moral strength is forged.

I will never forget the woman I met who spent her life curing teenagers of drug addiction. What, I asked her, did she do that made the difference to their lives? She replied, 'I'm probably the first person they've met who cared enough about them to say "No".' As she to them, so God to us.

38

Civility

The Yale law professor Steven L. Carter has just published a fascinating book entitled *Civility*. In it he tells the following story.

Carter is black and in 1966, when he was 10, he and his family moved into a white neighbourhood in Washington. It felt like exile. Along with his brothers and sisters, he sat on the front step, watching people passing by and waiting for someone to say 'Hello'. No one did. No word of greeting came. He felt invisible.

He describes his mood at the time. All his fears of how whites treat blacks were coming true. 'I knew we were not welcome here. I knew we would not be liked here. I knew we would have no friends here. I knew we should not have moved here.' Just then, a booming voice interrupted his thoughts. A white woman across the street, coming home from work, was calling out 'Welcome!' with a smile of obvious delight.

Disappearing into her house, she emerged a few minutes later with a tray piled high with cakes and brought this over to the children. Over the years, they became close, but it was that first gesture, writes Carter, which changed his world. It gave him a sense of belonging where there was none before. It made him realize that a black family could feel at home in a white area and that there could be relationships that were colour blind. A smile, a greeting, a spontaneous act of generosity broke down the wall of separation and turned strangers into friends.

Carter adds that the lady was a religious Jew. This leads him to speculate on the way faith shapes lives by alerting us to the affirmative duty of doing good. 'In the Jewish tradition,' he writes, 'this duty is captured in the requirement of *chesed* – the doing of acts of kindness – which is in turn derived from the understanding that human beings are made in the image of God … Civility itself may be seen as part of *chesed*: it does indeed require kindness toward our fellow citizens, including the ones who are strangers, and even when it is hard.'

Carter's book is important because it focuses on what he calls the prepolitical virtues, the things that bind us together as a society independently of political structures like governments, laws and courts. He is right to do so, because too little of our public discourse draws attention to what sustains our sense of participating in the common good.

The paradox of democratic politics is that it is an arena of conflict, yet it depends on a sense of community. Not only the majority but also minorities need to feel respected, safe in the knowledge that, though they may lose the vote, they will not lose their voice, their dignity or their rights. A decent society is one in which everyone feels they have a share. That depends on the careful cultivation of the virtues, from neighbourliness to self-sacrifice, which break down barriers between strangers and allow us to feel at home in the public square.

Carter calls religion 'the engine of civility' and doubts whether any other institution – the state, the market or the media – can generate that sense of being-for-others on which civil society depends. 'Nothing in contemporary secular conversation calls us to give up anything truly valuable for anybody else.' It took a simple act of generosity to restore Carter's sense of worth and belonging. The fabric of society is woven of such slender threads as these.

39

Confidences

Is anything private any more? Probably not, to judge by the latest round of political diaries, scandals and documentaries about the royal family.

Indiscretion pays. It boosts audience ratings and serialization rights. Woody Allen once joked, 'They threw me out for cheating in my metaphysics exam. They caught me looking into someone else's soul.' Today, looking into someone else's private life has become our favourite entertainment. Public figures now know that their most confidential remarks may eventually be broadcast to the world by people they once trusted. What, then, is left of friendship or honour?

I remember a dinner at which I was seated next to a distinguished academic whom I had asked to be a judge of an award scheme. The ceremony was due to take place the next week. 'Whatever you do,' I said, 'don't tell anyone the name of the winner. No one should know in advance.'

To my surprise, he proceeded loudly to name the person he and his fellow judges had chosen. 'But it's supposed to be a secret!' I said.

'I practise the Oxford way of keeping a secret,' he replied.

'What's that?'

'You only tell one person at a time!'

Luckily, on that occasion, no harm was done – but that is not always the case. Gossip rakes over the reputation of the dead.

It plays havoc with relationships between the living. Discretion is to speech what clothes are to the body. Too much nakedness, whether of the body or the soul, eventually makes us hateful to one another.

Judaism contains some of the most stringent rules ever formulated about the ethics of speech. The Bible commands, 'You shall not go as a gossip among your people.' Jewish law condemns 'evil speech' – speaking in a way that reflects badly on others – as a cardinal sin. One who shames a person in public is 'as if he shed his blood'.

Behind these judgements is a profound understanding of the power of speech. Just as God created the natural world by words ('And God said, Let there be...'), so we create the social world by words. A kind word heals. A cruel one injures – and psychological wounds cut deeper than physical ones. Judaism rejects the idea that 'words will never harm me'. Instead, the book of Proverbs says, 'Death and life are in the power of the tongue.'

Breaking confidences destroys the distinction between public and private. It treats strangers as if they were friends, and friends as if they were strangers. People in public life can now trust no one. That cannot be good for them, or in the long run for us.

Virtues such as honour and discretion are not meaningless. They were born in the desire to protect people, reputations and institutions. They cast a veil over the less lovely aspects of the human personality. Not every blemish need be held up to public view. A world in which people generally think well of one another is better than one in which we suspect that every saint is really a sinner. A cynical society is one that has lost the capacity to admire.

Words have power, and power without restraint eventually destroys those who wield it, as well as those against whom it is wielded. Not everything we think is something we should say. Not everything we say in private should be reported in public. Perhaps we need to reaffirm that most subtle of religious values – silence. It may lose us money, but it will gain us the trust of friends.

40

Rights and duties

The Hebrew Bible has no word for 'rights'. Instead, it is a book of duties. That is not to say that ancient Israel did not recognize the concept. Clearly it did. More than anywhere else, human rights owe their origin to the moral code of the Bible, above all to the idea that the human person is the image of God, the single most powerful idea in Western civilization. Nonetheless, the Bible has a different way of looking at rights, and it is one we might do well to recover.

Rights are things we claim. Duties are things we perform. Duties, in other words, are rights translated from the passive to the active mode. When we are young, we ask for things. We cannot get them ourselves. We are dependent. As we grow older, we learn to make things and share them. We learn reciprocity, on which all moral relationships depend. Clearly rights and duties are related. One person has a right to something only if others have a duty to provide it. There is nonetheless a difference between them. A rights-based culture tends to reduce us to a state of dependency. We make claims on others, assuming that they have the power. A duty-based culture is more mature. It asks us to give and to be sensitive to the needs of others. In its most religious expression, it recognizes that what we possess, we do not own. It has been entrusted to us and one of the conditions of that trust is that we share some of it with others in need.

That is why the Hebrew word *tzedakah*, normally translated as 'charity', actually means 'justice'. Charity is what we give out of the goodness of our heart. Justice is what we give because we must, because equity is one of the conditions of God's blessing and because we cannot eat in freedom while others around us are going hungry.

The concept of rights has an honourable history. It was invented to protect people from the power of the state. It set limits to what governments could do. The fundamental rights were those to life, property and certain personal freedoms such as speech and association, and to infringe those was to transgress the boundaries of legitimate power. The social contract meant that governments came into being to protect citizens from one another, to create order and the rule of law. Any government which deprived citizens of the very freedoms it was created to protect thereby forfeited its authority. In this sense, rights are important. They defend the individual by setting a boundary to the state. When we use the concept more widely, however, it creates a distorted view of the moral life.

There is a fascinating detail in Jewish law. Judaism has an elaborate set of rules of *tzedakah* – that word that means more than charity; perhaps 'welfare' would be a fair translation. One states the following: a community must provide a poor person not only with the means to live, but also with enough so that he too can give to others. Rationally this makes no sense. The money will be given to the poor anyway. Why give it to one person to give to another? Psychologically, on the other hand, it makes very good sense indeed. Giving is an essential part of dignity. Judaism sees it as no less than a human need. That is why even those who have to receive also have to be able to give. They must be in a position not just to claim their rights but also to fulfil their duties to others.

In general, the ability to do one's share is part of an inclusive society. One of the deepest forms of belonging is to be able to look at something and say, 'I helped build this.' That is what a duty-based culture gives us. It turns us from paying guests into builders. It sees us as co-creators of the common good. The Hebrew Bible was wise when it spoke of duties rather than rights. A giving culture is healthier and happier than a demanding one.

PART VII

Communities of Faith

41

Community

The other day a man I knew was attacked and beaten up in the street. He was coming home from synagogue when a group of youths set upon him, knocked him down and started kicking him. I heard about it a few days later and phoned him up, expecting to find him in a state of shock. To my amazement, he said, 'The police have just come round to take the details. I told them what happened, but I had to add something. I said, "I know this is going to sound strange, but I'd like to thank my attackers. They showed me the friends I didn't know I had."'

Having struggled home, bruised and dishevelled, he went to lie down to recover from the shock. Somehow his neighbours heard about it. The next day, at early morning prayers in the synagogue, the news got around. From then on he was besieged by well-wishers. Some brought gifts of food. Others dropped in to see how he was. The phone rang incessantly. Prayers were said for his recovery. He found himself surrounded by a network of concern. It should not have surprised him. He had done this many times for other people when they were going through a crisis of their own, but it was the first time he had been on the receiving end and he suddenly realized how strong were the bonds of support that surrounded him. That is what community is. It is society on a human scale, where they notice when you are missing and take the trouble to find out why. It is where you are there for other people and they are there for you. It is where your griefs are halved and your celebrations doubled by being shared.

Judaism is an insistently communal faith. There have been belief systems that emphasized the individual. Dean Inge once defined religion as 'what an individual does with his own solitude'. Walter Savage Landor called solitude the 'audience chamber of God'. Plotinus spoke of the 'flight of the alone to the Alone'. For them the primary religious experience is the private communion of the soul with God. That has never been the Jewish way. To be sure, we have had our share of mystics and contemplatives, but the greatest challenge as Judaism has seen it is not to ascend from earth to heaven through the journey of the soul, but to bring the Divine presence from heaven to earth and share it with others. That is an essentially collective task, which is why the covenant at Mount Sinai was made not with individuals but with an entire people. In biblical times it was the task of a nation. In the Diaspora it became the function of communities.

So we pray together, celebrate together, confess our sins together, even mourn together. The holiest prayers in Judaism require a quorum, minimally defined as 10 men. The sages ruled that 'one who separates himself from the community' forfeits his share in the world to come. Moses Maimonides defines this as simply living apart from others, not sharing their burdens or their grief. One who separates him- or herself from the community may lead a life of righteousness, but he or she leads it alone, and that is not the Jewish way.

It is at moments of distress that you understand why. To face a crisis is one thing; to face it alone is another. There is by now an enormous literature spreading across several disciplines to show how important it is to a person's wellbeing to be surrounded by friends. Merely having people to talk to makes a difference. We speak of 'unburdening' ourselves to others, and the metaphor is exact. There is something about human nature that makes troubles shared easier to bear. We are, as Aristotle and Maimonides said, social animals. What distinguishes *homo sapiens* from other life forms is the extent and complexity of our sociality.

One of the researchers who discovered that regular attendance at a place of worship added years to life expectancy hazarded a guess as to why. People who do so, he said, 'have friends and a sense of importance in the scheme of things'. He is probably right. Faith makes a difference, and the biggest difference it makes is in sustaining the bonds between people. Faith lives in communities. They are the human face of the Divine reality that tells us we are not alone.

42

Trust and the Prisoner's Dilemma

One of the most exciting intellectual developments in years has come from the application of games theory to sociobiology. What is fascinating is the question it sets out to solve, one already asked by Charles Darwin over a century ago. Where does altruism come from? If evolution is the story of the selfish gene, how do we so often come to act selflessly?

Two things helped sociobiologists move towards an answer. The first was a device in games theory called the Prisoner's Dilemma. Two suspects are arrested by the police. They have some evidence against them but not enough. They separate the two prisoners and offer them a deal. If one co-operates by informing against his friend, he gets off free, while the other gets 10 years in prison. If neither co-operate, they each get one year on a lesser charge. If both inform, both get five years. What is the logical thing for either prisoner to do?

Self-interest suggests: inform. That way you either go free or get five years in prison. You avoid the worst outcome and have a chance of the best. Taken together, though, their best interest is served by neither prisoner co-operating. That way, each gets only one year. The trouble is, they cannot communicate. They are kept apart. Under those conditions, self-interest defeats collective interest.

The Prisoner's Dilemma neatly states the problem of rational action. I can work out what is best for me when only I am involved, but normally the outcome of a situation will depend on the responses of others and I cannot predict what they will be. So I work out the alternatives and choose the one that offers me the best range of outcomes. The trouble is, what is best for me is not best for us. It is not even as good for me as the outcome I could achieve if only I could secure co-operation. How, then, do we create the possibility of collective action? It depends on trust. I can only act for the common good if the other person keeps his or her side of the bargain. But how does trust arise? Self-interest dictates that I take advantage of the other person whenever I can. Between two people who consistently act to maximize their own advantage, trust and co-operative action cannot be born.

What finally broke through this dilemma was a computer programme devised in the 1970s by Robert Axelrod. This simulated a world populated by different species, each of which had a different way of solving the Prisoner's Dilemma. He offered a prize to the programme that did best in repeated encounters. The winner – devised by game theorist Anatol Rapoport – was called Tit-for-Tat. What it showed was that aggressive strategies worked in the short run but not the long. Co-operation eventually wins against self-interest. Tit-for-Tat was later superseded by yet better programmes, but what they had in common was reciprocal altruism: if you behave well to me, I will behave well to you. The more effective programmes also introduced the concept of forgiveness. Negative reciprocity – if you do bad to me, I will do bad to you – is powerful in deterring aggression, but it can also lock individuals into a destructive cycle of retaliation, which only forgiveness breaks.

These theories tell us why communities are important. Self-interest works for one round of the Prisoner's Dilemma, but not for a whole series of them. In the long run, successful outcomes depend on co-operation. That has to be built on trust, and trust has to be earned over repeated encounters. This is why communities, where we get to know people and spend extended time in their company, are where altruism is found. Crime, incivility and aggression are higher in cities than in villages, and higher still in places where the population is transient, for the obvious reason that we are unlikely to meet the victim again. They are like a single round of the Prisoner's Dilemma. We do what is best for me, not us.

Nothing so conduces to virtue as prolonged exposure to the same set of people. We learn the rules of co-operation, the habits of altruism. We discover that I am best served by caring for you as you are by active concern for me. Self-interest and selflessness merge. Communities are workshops of virtue, not by what they teach but by what they are: places where we meet, get to know each other and eventually learn that we can depend on one another. They are where trust is born.

43

Bowling alone

When people start philosophizing about something, it is a sure sign that it is getting lost. Much recent social thought has been 'communitarian'. Thinkers on both sides of the Atlantic have emphasized the way in which communities are a vital part of our social ecology. They are where we gain our identity, preserve our traditions, establish friendships and develop reciprocity, the give-and-take on which social life depends. They are where we learn to speak the 'we' as against the 'I'-inflected language of consumerism and a rights-based political culture. A community is like the ark of the ancient Israelites, about which Jewish tradition said, 'Those who carried it discovered that it was carrying them.'

Communities are in short supply in the modern world. Between the 1970s and the 1990s there was a marked decline in attendance at public meetings and membership of civic and cultural groups. Repeatedly, surveys of children have shown them to be less interested in politics than their parents, and more interested in personal relationships and private lives. The Harvard political scientist Robert Putnam gave the phenomenon a name. Noting that more Americans went bowling than ever before, but fewer joined teams, he called it 'bowling alone'.

Not everyone has accepted his thesis. Certainly there has been a growth in other forms of association – therapeutic groups, self-help gatherings, voluntary organizations – but they lack the ongoing engagement with a stable set of others that communities once represented. Therapeutic encounters are ways in which I get others to listen to me talking about myself. Voluntary organizations often involve helping others removed from me in locality and lifestyle, and there is a difference between the people I help and those with whom I live. Many of today's groups involve no long-term commitment. I go for as long as I find it interesting, then I leave and join something else. These things are valuable, but they do not replicate the texture or yield the satisfactions of a life lived with others.

The reasons for the decline are clear. In the past, communities were often formed on the basis of long-standing geographical proximity. People stayed in the same place for a long time, so they got to know their neighbours. Today we move. The very anonymity of urban life diminishes trust. We are afraid to leave the door open. We are not quite sure whether the person coming up to us in the street wants to wish us well or steal our watch. We become more guarded, suspicious and defensive. We move within a narrow circle of friends. That means that we tend to meet the people like us and no longer, as we once did, people from different age, income and occupational groups. Outside our circle the world is increasingly unknown. We learn about it from distant glimpses on television or in the press, and our anxieties are easily aroused. Ignorance feeds fear. The world beyond our front door becomes a threatening place.

It may well be that, schools aside, congregations have become the last great refuge of community. Certainly the evidence from the United States is striking. Princeton sociologist Robert Wuthnow reports that in answer to the question, 'If someone in your family became seriously ill, who could you count on for help?' 86 per cent of regular attenders replied that it would be someone in their congregation; 50 per cent said someone at work; 35 per cent referred to public agencies. The religiously committed were more likely to have helped a neighbour, voted in local elections, attended neighbourhood meetings, contributed to charitable appeals and performed voluntary work.

Communities are an essential part of collective wellbeing. They bridge the gap between family and society. They are large enough to extend our sympathies but small enough to be intelligible. They are the human face of the common good, which would otherwise remain as an abstraction. They are where we learn to be citizens, carrying our share of the collective weight. Freedom is the art of association, and it is in communities that we learn it.

44

Turning strangers into friends

I used to love those Sabbaths in our synagogue in the West End. You never knew who would be there. It was set in the heart of London's hotel district, so our congregation was always full of tourists. There would be businessmen from New York, *kibbutzniks* from Israel, travellers from Turkey, Mexico, Brazil. Often, welcoming our visitors and finding out where they were from, we would find two couples from the same town in Italy or the same suburb in Los Angeles who had never met before and had come thousands of miles to discover neighbours they never knew they had. Each Friday I used to recite the afternoon prayer with special fervour when I reached the paragraph that speaks of God 'sounding the great ram's horn for our freedom' and gathering Jews together 'from the four corners of the earth'. There is something about the synagogue and the Sabbath, I thought, that turns strangers into friends.

That, for me, is the beauty of a community of faith. It cuts across boundaries. It brings together what other institutions keep apart. In one synagogue where I used to worship there were several millionaires. Sitting alongside them was the man who sold newspapers in Piccadilly Circus, and another who lived alone and always turned up with holes in his shoes and patches on his clothes. In another synagogue, close to where we live, a Conservative peer used to pray a few feet away from a Labour Cabinet Minister. There was always a fair sprinkling of lively people in their eighties and nineties. Somehow, the synagogue kept them young. They would come each week, and often each day, to give thanks for being alive and as often as not to exchange the latest gossip on who had fallen out with whom. Of course there were also the children, to me the most important people – two-, three- and four-year-olds, for whom I always kept a store of sweets, remembering the rabbi in the synagogue I used to go to when I was three, who used to give me two oval sweets with stars on the wrappers to ease the walk home.

What brought us together? Not power or exchange. Not pursuit of interest or advantage. Just the need regularly to remind ourselves of who we are, what we belong to, the faith we share, the story of which our lives are a part, the ideals we have inherited from the past, the values that frame our lives and give them meaning and purpose. At a Jewish wedding, the bride and groom stand together under the bridal canopy, symbol of the home they will build. In our prayers we speak of God's 'canopy of peace', and that is what the synagogue spreads over us, sheltering us under its shade, gathering us in its embrace.

There is nothing abstract about the faith we share. We know, pretty well, what it demands of us. It asks us to take responsibility for one another. We know that people will be there for us when we need them, sharing our celebrations, comforting us when we are bereaved, visiting us when we are ill, helping us when we are in trouble. We know, too, that we have to be there for others when they need us. We take special delight in the great moments of life, when a child is born or reaches the age of maturity – *bar mitzvah* for boys, *bat mitzvah* for girls – when a couple get engaged or married or celebrate an anniversary. These are not private celebrations. They are moments when the whole community takes part, because it knows it is being renewed. The synagogue, like other places of worship in other faiths, is about the 'we' not the 'I'. It is the human face of the Divine presence. Being part of a community, I know what it is not to be alone, what it is to feel: 'I will fear no evil for you are with me.'

All of us who are part of the community know our individual failings, yet while we are there we are lifted into something greater than any of us could achieve alone. We are part of an ancient story, voices in a choral symphony, participants in something more gracious than the world outside with its conflicts and collisions. It is not that these do not matter. It is just that they are not all that is. Somehow we need those places that strengthen the bonds between us, teaching us to value one another and give thanks for what we have. Politics and economics are about resolving conflicts between strangers. Our places of worship are about turning strangers into friends.

45

Where they know my name

As Chief Rabbi, I spend much of my time visiting communities throughout Britain and the Commonwealth. Wherever I go, I am usually asked to speak – probably on average more than 200 speeches a year. I always work hard at preparation and try to say something thought provoking. What always brings me down to earth is the response. After I have spoken, I take time to mix with the people there, and they always have questions to ask. The surprising thing is that, almost invariably, the question is the same, no matter what the subject of my talk has been. It comes in a dozen variations, but it always adds up to this: 'Do you know me?' 'I recognize you, but do you recognize me?' 'Do you know my name?'

Is this, I wonder, a specifically Jewish question? Are we so small a people that we assume everyone knows everyone else? (I love the story about the advertising campaign in New York. Throughout the city large posters announced, 'You have a friend in the Chase Manhattan Bank.' Underneath one, someone had written, 'But in the Bank of Israel you have family!' Jews are, in more ways than one, a large and boisterous extended family.)

The psychologist Abraham Maslow suggests, though, that the need to be recognized is universal. We have physical needs, for food, shelter and security. Beyond these we have psychological needs, the deepest of which is to be known and valued for what we uniquely are. Eventually I realized that this was a major part of my work, to communicate not only ideas but also a sense of worth to the many people who make up our communities. There may be several hundred people in the room, and I may have only an hour to spare, but while I am talking to someone he or she must be the one person in my universe. That may be the most important thing I can give. Ideas can be found in books, but a sense of value and recognition can only be had from other people, and it matters. A sense of worth, affirmed by others, is a source of moral energy, perhaps the most potent there is.

One of my favourite places is the Israel Museum in Jerusalem. It houses a magnificent collection of works of art, exhibits from the Diaspora, and ancient artefacts from prebiblical Canaan. But there is one object there, smaller than the rest, that fills me with awe. It is a tiny piece of parchment dating from the First Temple, more than 2,500 years ago. This is the oldest surviving fragment of a biblical text, written in a Hebrew script that had already become obsolete by the time of the Dead Sea Scrolls. What makes it fascinating is that it contains 15 Hebrew words still said today as they were written then – the priestly blessings: 'May the Lord bless you and keep you. May the Lord make His face shine upon you and be gracious to you. May the Lord turn His face towards you and give you peace.' It is astonishing to see those words, so familiar yet so ancient, preserved across half the history of human civilization on a scrap of leather, perhaps an amulet, owned by someone who walked in the courtyards of King Solomon's Temple.

It was only after my experience of visiting communities that I understood the last of those blessings. What does it mean for God to 'turn His face towards you'? And how does that 'give you peace'? What is revolutionary about the Bible is the idea that God is a person, not a power. That means that He knows us and cares about us. There is a line in the Psalms that says, 'He counts the number of the stars and gives each a name.' An impersonal Big Bang could give rise to a billion galaxies, but only a person can give something a name.

God knows us not abstractly but personally and intimately. He turns His face towards us, He values us as individuals. He knows our name. There is no greater source of peace – peace of the soul – than this, knowing that we are known, recognizing that we are recognized. Then I understood how community is the human expression of Divine love. It is where I am valued simply for who I am, how I live and what I give to others. It is the place where they know my name.

PART VIII

Faith and Friendship

46

The dignity of difference

The good news: faith creates communities. The bad news: those communities often collide. More wars have been fought in the name of God than in any other cause. Is this not a refutation of faith, or at least a terrible indictment of it?

Of course it is. The problem, I suspect, has less to do with faith than with community and its Siamese twin, identity. We define who we are by saying who we are not. The circle of concern has an inside and an outside: those who are like us and those who are different. Pride leads us to attach great, even ultimate, significance to that distinction. God, we say, is with us, not them. They become the infidel, the unredeemed. From there it is a short step to invoking God to justify war. We are fighting His battle for the sake of His truth. What He has to say, we do not stop to ask. In the cry of battle it is hard to hear the still, small voice of peace.

Yet if religion is the problem, it is also the solution. Monotheism was the first system in world history to postulate the fatherhood of God and thus the brotherhood of mankind. As Francis Fukuyama puts it, 'It is religion alone that first suggested that the final community within which its moral rules should apply ... should be mankind itself.' Religions were the force that turned families into tribes, tribes into nations and nations into civilizations. They enlarge our radius of concern.

There is something else, however, obvious yet rarely noted, in which Judaism holds a special place. Alone among monotheisms, it worships the universal God but in a particularistic way. This is a fact of immense significance, and it is set out in the Bible in a simple way.

You do not have to read far to realize that it is the story of a particular people, Israel. Yet the Bible does not start, as it should, with the birth of that people. It begins with a brief history of humanity as a whole – Adam and Eve, Cain and Abel, Noah and the Flood, archetypes of the prehistory of mankind. Then comes the Tower of Babel, the confusion of languages and the multiplicity of cultures. Only then does Abraham appear and the history of the covenantal people begin. What is the point of this story?

Western philosophy has been described as 'a series of footnotes to Plato', and in a real sense Plato marked out one of the great ways of understanding reality. He was, we know, fascinated by the problem of knowledge. How could you know what a chair or table was if, down here on earth, all chairs were different, all tables constantly getting bashed and broken? His answer was to seek knowledge in a world of forms where all chairs were alike and never changed. Truth was timeless and universal. That, for much of history, has been the philosophical quest.

The Hebrew Bible tells the opposite story. God lives not in a Platonic heaven but down here on earth in all its diversity and change. Universal civilizations do not work. They begin by crushing diversity and end by killing people who are different. That is why God chooses first a family, then a people, and commands them to be different. Only a world that has space for difference is one that honours the creation of God and the creativity of mankind. In so doing He posed two challenges: to Jews and those among whom they live. Do Jews have the courage to be different? Do others have the generosity to tolerate difference? When the first fails, the result is assimilation. When the second fails, the result is anti-Semitism. Both have constantly threatened Jewish survival – but Jews survive.

There is one God, and there are many faiths. That tells us that God is bigger than religion, even though we need religion to speak to God. Religions are like languages. The existence of English does not refute, replace or supersede the existence of French, Italian or Urdu. Each language preserves a unique set of sensibilities. There are things you can say in one that you cannot translate, without loss, into others. That is why we are enlarged by their multiplicity and would be impoverished if one disappeared. Nonetheless, they describe the same reality, as religions reach out to the one God. They do not, should not, threaten one another. To believe otherwise is to mistake religion for God. A distinguished scientist once wrote to *The Times* and said that all religions teach different things; all claim to be true; all are therefore false, because each is refuted by the others. What he forgot was Niels Bohr's great insight: 'The opposite of a correct statement is a false statement. But the opposite of a profound truth may well be another profound truth.'

The great challenge to religions in a global age is whether, at last, they can make space for one another, recognizing God's image in someone who is not in my image, God's voice when it speaks in someone else's language. At stake is the great teaching of the Hebrew Bible – the diversity of creation, the dignity of difference.

47

A new way

Rabbi Hayyim of Sens, the nineteenth-century sage, told the following parable.

A man was lost in a forest. For days he had tried to find a way out. Each time, he failed. Close to despair, he heard a noise. Looking up, he saw a stranger coming towards him. 'Now I will be saved, for surely he knows the way out.'

But the stranger approached him and said, 'Friend, do not ask me the way out, for I too am lost. But this I can tell you. Do not go the way I have come, for it too will lead you astray. And now, let us search for a new way together.'

That, for me, is the story of the millennium. Looking back over the past 1,000 years, one theme dominates: religious persecution, the readiness of people of God to inflict suffering in the name of God. Were I to give it a starting point, I would go back to 1096 and the First Crusade. It was then that religious difference turned murderous. On their way to the Holy Land, the Christian soldiers paused to inflict bloodshed on Jewish communities. There were massacres throughout France and the Rhineland. Some historians estimate that as many as one third of Jews in these regions were killed.

It was the beginning of one of the darkest chapters in the history of faith. From then on the condition of Jews in Europe steadily worsened. The story of the Middle Ages, told from a Jewish standpoint, is a tale of inquisitions, expulsions, persecutions and pogroms. European Jewish history is written in tears.

The answer that spoke to many was simple. If religion leads to bloodshed, then the absence of religion will lead to human dignity and freedom. It was a compelling answer, but the wrong one. Secular tyrannies proved even worse than religious ones. Hitler's Germany and Stalin's Russia stand as eternal warnings against a world in which people worship not God but the state. Idols demand human sacrifice and their hunger is insatiable.

Yet if we search for a symbol of hope, we find it here and now. In the Middle Ages, England was Europe's leader in anti-Jewish persecution. The first blood libel – in which Jews were falsely, indeed obscenely, accused of murdering Christian children for religious ends – took place in Norwich in 1144. One of the great massacres of Jews took place in York in 1190. In 1290 England became the first country in Europe to expel its Jews. Where England led, other countries followed.

It was precisely England, however, in a later age, that led the world in religious tolerance. It was Cromwell in 1655 who readmitted Jews. It was John Locke in the seventeenth century who laid the foundations of religious toleration. Under Churchill, Britain fought one of the great battles of all time for human freedom. If anyone doubts that nations change, England is the proof.

Today the great faith communities meet in mutual respect and dignity. Dialogue has replaced disputation. Friendship has taken the place of suspicion. That is a momentous achievement, and it lights the path to the future.

We now know that nothing was ever achieved by intolerance. Faith lives in generosity. Stripped of power, religion survives only by influence, by its ability to set before us living examples of high ideals, supportive communities and holy lives. Perhaps we have learned, too, that the multiplicity of faiths is not a tragedy but the gift of God, who is closer to us than we are to ourselves and yet lives in lives quite different from ours. We have sought, and found, a better way.

48

Who best values others?

Some years ago, in the course of a television documentary, Prince Charles made the famous statement that he would like to become 'Defender of Faith' rather than 'Defender of *the* Faith'. At the time, the phrase caused a flurry of controversy, but it deserves more serious reflection than it has received.

How can the future head of the Church of England be a defender of other faiths which are not his own? Yet how can a future monarch not defend the integrity of the many faith communities that make up contemporary Britain? Is there a way through this impasse? I think there is.

Many years ago when I was a student, I met one of the great rabbis of the twentieth century. At that time I was at a crossroads in my own religious development, and I asked him the following question. 'I would like to become a more committed Jew, but I also value the world outside – the great music, art and literature whose inspiration is often drawn from quite un-Jewish sources. Must I make this sacrifice? Is religious commitment exclusive?'

He replied with a parable: 'There were once two men who spent their lives transporting stones. One carried rocks, the other diamonds. One day they were given emeralds to carry. The man who had spent his days carrying rocks saw emeralds as just another heavy weight, a burden of no intrinsic value. The one who had carried diamonds recognized emeralds as another form of precious stone, different, but with their own distinctive beauty. So it is with faith. If your own faith is nothing more than a burden, you will not value the faith of others. But if you cherish your faith, you will value other people's faith also, even though it is different from your own. You will know that faiths are like jewels. One is especially your own, but all are precious.'

It was a wise answer, and I have tried to live by it ever since. Many times I have met and been moved by sincere Christians, Muslims, Hindus, Sikhs and Buddhists. There is something unmistakable about people whose lives have been touched by the sense of mystery at the heart of the universe. You feel it in their serenity, graciousness or inner poise. It can be a smile that gathers you into its embrace, or a laugh that lifts you above the pain and conflict of the world, or a love that surprises you by its generosity. Such people leave you feeling affirmed and enlarged.

At a level beyond words, faith sends out its light to faith. Those who recognize it in themselves can sense it in others. Just as a painter may find inspiration in the work of artists far removed in time and style from his own, so a believer can feel reinforced by the distant echoes of the Divine presence in other traditions, other lives. It does not weaken my faith to know that others find God in different ways. Instead, it strengthens my conviction that God is beyond the particularities of language, time and culture, always surprising us by being where we least expect Him to be.

Far from being paradoxical, it makes a great deal of sense to say that one who defends a particular faith is best poised to defend other faiths as well. If we had to entrust our most cherished possession to someone else to guard, who would we choose? Someone, surely, who has treasures of his own and therefore knows the value of what he has to defend.

49

When we cannot worship together

Your daughter comes in one day. She is crying. She has suffered an emotional hurt. A teacher has said an unkind word, or she has failed an exam, or someone she thought was a friend has turned out not to be one after all. Her world has been shaken and she needs your help. You give her a hug. You tell her she is great. You explain that things like this happen. You see her smile through the tears. Moments like this are among the most important we can have with our children. They give them the strength to believe in themselves and carry on. That is part of what parenthood is.

Now imagine that in the middle of the conversation a friend rings at the door and comes in. She was just passing by and decided to say hello. You can do two things. You can explain to your friend that now is not a good time, or you can ask your daughter to be patient and wait. One thing you cannot do: you cannot continue the conversation in the presence of someone else. It is too intimate. It belongs to the special bond between parent and child. It is too close to be shared by someone else.

Does this compromise your relationship with your friend? I do not think so. You like her, trust her, you do things together. You know that you can count on her and she on you. Your friendship is real, and part of what makes it real is that you and she both know that there are moments when you need to be together with members of your family, sharing words that can only be said within the family.

There are different kinds of love. There is love between husbands and wives. There is love between parents and children. There is love between friends. There is love that can sometimes spring up between strangers. Each has its own contours, its own level of intensity, its own place in life. One of the unwritten rules of friendship is that it knows its limits. There are things we can say to our children or our parents that we cannot say to our friends. A good friend knows this. That is what makes him or her a friend.

One of the most blessed transformations in recent years has been the relationship between faiths. Religions that had been hostile to one another for centuries have become friends. Does that mean, inevitably, that we can and should worship together? And if not, does that mean that we cannot really be friends?

Jews and Christians speak of God as a parent – 'our Father'. That is a metaphor, but it reflects a powerful experience in the life of faith. It means that when we stand in prayer, we discard the masks we wear at other times, the roles we play, the distances we keep. We speak to God in total intimacy. We bring Him our pain, our distress, our hopes and fears. He puts His arm around us and gives us strength. At that moment God is not a stranger or even a friend. He is a parent offering us unconditional love.

A house of worship is a home. Our several faiths are separate families, and each has its own language of intimacy with God. There is a difference between family and friends, and true friends know and respect that difference. Perhaps one day all faiths will join to become one family. Then, surely, we will worship together. Until then, however, let us give thanks that at least we can be friends.

50

Remembering Sir Isaiah

Reading Michael Ignatieff's delightful biography of the late Sir Isaiah Berlin, I was struck yet again by the inadequacy, if not the downright mischief, of words like 'secular' and 'religious'.

Sir Isaiah, one of the truly great minds of the twentieth century, used to see himself as a 'secular' Jew. He once said to me, with a smile, 'Chief Rabbi, don't talk to me about religion. When it comes to God, I'm tone deaf.'

He even used to tease me about my own faith. How could I, a trained philosopher, be a believing Jew? 'If it helps,' I said, 'think of me as a lapsed heretic.' He chuckled in that lovely, deep-throated way of his and we declared a truce.

Yet, despite his professed agnosticism, he faithfully kept at least some of Judaism's religious rituals. On High Holy Days he attended synagogue. He observed the annual memorial for his late father. He used to conduct the Seder service on Passover at which we tell the story of the exodus of the Israelites from slavery. When he knew he was about to die, he requested a religious funeral. Officiating on that occasion was one of my most moving experiences. He was a man I admired. I miss him still.

There are many people, like Sir Isaiah, who have a deep respect for the heritage of faith – its history, traditions and rituals, its texts, music and holy days – without necessarily seeing themselves as 'religious'. Are they, or are they not, secular?

To my mind, the question highlights a confusion between

religion and spirituality. They are two quite different things. Spirituality is the poetry of the soul. Religion is the prose. Spirituality is the direct encounter with God. Religion is the behaviour we adopt when we express our sense of belonging to a group who, at a key point in its history, encountered the Divine. You can be spiritual without being religious. You can be religious without being spiritual. It is almost like the distinction between love and marriage. Love is an emotion. Marriage is an institution. They are linked, but they are not the same.

One of the great shortcomings of our time is that we have come to value emotions at the expense of institutions. We place a higher value on love than marriage. We seek spirituality rather than religion. In the meantime we forget why, for much of human history, people have sought to create and protect institutions.

The reason is that they give permanence to what is fleeting, stability to the mercurial, public expression to what would otherwise be private. We cannot spend our lives speaking poetry alone. Marriage is not less beautiful for its prosaic passages – the shopping, the laundry, the shared routine. Nor is religion less beautiful for its more routine moments – the daily prayers, the regular rituals. Reading John Bayley's moving account of life with Iris Murdoch after she had contracted Alzheimer's disease convinced me that sometimes the most mundane acts within a marriage shine with their own moral beauty. In this respect, religion is like being married to the Divine presence. It is about the long stretches of loyalty between the moments of high passion.

Sir Isaiah, tone deaf to God, still enjoyed the music of religious ritual. He respected Judaism even if he could not fully share its sense of the Divine. Perhaps he simply knew what we sometimes forget: that marriage is more than love; religion is more than spirituality. He was not a believing Jew, but he was a loyal one, and that is no small thing.

51

Cardinal Hume

When I think of Cardinal Hume, I recall the words of Judaism's early sages. They asked, 'Who is a hero?' They answered, 'One who turns strangers into friends.' That was his great gift. He drew people to him by his love of God and his deep feeling for humanity. While you were with him you felt enlarged. He was a friend, and we were lucky to have him.

He achieved things that were thought to be impossible. He spoke of God in a secular age and was listened to. He articulated clear moral values and his words shone through the relativistic mist. He took principled political stands and was respected for it. In an age of celebrities he showed that humility – that forgotten virtue – has a power and presence of its own.

He was loved by Christians of all denominations, but he achieved something else of historic significance. More than anyone else besides the Pope, he brought reconciliation and friendship between Catholics and Jews. For centuries relations between the two faiths had been tense. Jews had suffered under the Catholic Church. Especially after the Holocaust, there was much healing to be done. Cardinal Hume achieved it, as he did so much else, by the force of his personality, and by his ability to hear pain and speak gently to it.

We became friends. The source of his feelings for Judaism and the Jewish people was twofold. He had reflected deeply on the Holocaust. It was, to him, a wound in the flesh of humanity.

He felt the need for a new way, and took every opportunity to visit the Jewish community and identify with it. On one occasion, probably without precedent, he joined the Archbishop of Canterbury to attend a service at the Bevis Marks Synagogue in the City of London for the fiftieth anniversary of VE Day. In one of our last conversations he told me how much he cherished the memory of that moment when he joined with the Jewish community in prayer.

His other attachment was to the Jewish roots of Christianity itself. He loved the book of Psalms and looked on it as one of the sources of his own spirituality. He never forgot that the first Christians were Jews, and that much of their vision and vocabulary came from the Hebrew Bible. A few months before he died, we were discussing the millennium. I reminded the Cardinal that it was a Christian celebration, not a Jewish one. 'But, Chief Rabbi,' he replied with his angelic smile, 'if it hadn't been for you, there wouldn't be an us!'

What did he teach us, people of all faiths and those of none? He taught us three things above all. He showed us that moral relativism is not the only answer to a complex, changing world. When the winds blow hardest, it is then that you need strong roots. He spoke insistently of the sanctity of life. He warned against the encroachments of abortion and euthanasia. In his battles for the Guildford Four and the Birmingham Six, he showed an almost biblical passion for justice. In his last great campaign, for international debt relief, he reminded us that the obligations of the rich to the poor apply all the more strongly in a global economy. These, for him, were not opinions but objective truths and he spoke with the rare authority that comes from a life of reverence and obedience.

He taught us, too, that religion's obituary is premature. Faith lives on in a faithless age. As Philip Larkin put it,

And that much can never be obsolete
Since someone will forever be surprising
A hunger in himself to be more serious.

Beneath the noise of a consumer and computer society, people still strain to hear the music. Cardinal Hume was a man of God because he was a man of the people. He knew, and showed, that at its highest, love of God is love of humanity. The search for God is the search for meaning, discovered, not invented. As our world becomes more fragmented, so our need grows for an overarching vision of the dignity of the personal – the idea at the heart of Judaism and Christianity. This is a truth taught best not through theology but personal example. God needs living witnesses, and the Cardinal was one.

Not least, he showed that religion can be a force for reconciliation. That is no small achievement as we reach the end of a millennium in which, too often, people have fought and persecuted others in the name of God. The great religious figures of our century – I think of Martin Buber, Martin Luther King and the Dalai Lama – have known that we find the Divine presence at the very core of our humanity, where what is most unique about us is also the most universal. The Cardinal knew that those whose faith is deepest reach the point where, transcending boundaries, soul speaks to soul. Out of that conversation true peace is born.

Serene in life, serene in the face of death, Cardinal Hume was a man of God who turned strangers into friends.

PART IX

From Optimism to Hope

52

Losing our way

'Thank God,' says the sage, stroking his beard and looking up from his volume of Talmud, 'things are good.' Then he pauses, thinks a while, and adds, 'But tell me one thing, Master of the Universe ... if things are so good, how come they're so bad?' That, surely, is the question of our time.

We approach the new millennium on the cusp of extraordinary possibilities. Never in history have we had so much freedom and affluence, so much diversity and choice, as we do today in the liberal democracies of the West. The average shopper in the average supermarket is confronted with an array of goods that a century ago would have been beyond the dreams of the wealthiest king. Journeys that, a lifetime ago, would have taken months today take hours. We have sent space probes to the most distant planets, photographed the birth of galaxies, fathomed the origins of the universe and decoded the biological structure of life itself. The frontiers of human possibility extend daily.

The speed of advance in the twentieth century defies comparison with anything else in the long history of progress. By the beginning of the century there had still been no successful attempt at one of man's oldest dreams – powered flight. Today space shuttles are routine. The twentieth century has been the century of radio, television, the computer, the Internet, the laser beam, the credit card, artificial intelligence, satellite communication, organ transplantation and microsurgery. We have achieved immediate global communication and the instant satisfaction of desires.

Coincidentally with these advances, however, throughout the West there has been an unprecedented rise in depressive illness, suicide and suicide attempts, drug and alcohol abuse, violence and crime. Crime rates have risen 1,000 per cent in 40 years. Since the 1960s, in virtually all the liberal democracies of the West, divorce rates have risen six times, the number of children born outside marriage has risen five times, the number of children living with a lone parent has risen three times.

These changes have not been without a price. We worry. So do our children. Theirs has become a confused and confusing world. In the United States, every three hours gun violence takes a child's life. Every nine minutes a child is arrested for a drug or alcohol offence. Every minute an American teenager has a baby. Every 26 seconds a child runs away from home.

One of the most telling indicators of what has changed came in a comparison between schools in 1940 and 1990. Teachers were asked the following question: 'What are the seven most serious problems you encounter among your pupils?' In 1940 the answers were these: talking out of turn, chewing gum, making noise, running in corridors, cutting in line, not wearing school uniform, dropping litter. In 1990, in reply to the same question, teachers answered: drug abuse, alcohol abuse, teenage pregnancy, suicide, rape, robbery, assault.

Why, if things are so good, are they so bad? The shortest, simplest answer is that we have lost our way. We have focused on the how but not the why. In achieving material abundance we have begun to lose our moral and spiritual bearings. In achieving technical mastery we have lost sight of the question – to what end? Valuing science at the expense of ethics, we have unparalleled knowledge of what is and unprecedented doubts about what ought to be.

Luckily, all that we have lost is recoverable. We are not prisoners of time because we have the databanks of collective memory through which the past speaks to the present and guides it on its way. The human spirit is unique in its capacity to correct its own errors. What we damage, we can repair. What we destroy, we can rebuild. There is one proviso: that we do not lose our sense of hope.

53

Sifting hope from ashes

The toughest assignment I ever faced was my first visit to Auschwitz. I had been asked to go there by the BBC. Each year, just before the Jewish New Year, I make a television programme, a kind of Jewish message to the nation. In 1995, 50 years after the end of World War II and the liberation of the camps, the BBC felt that this should be the subject of the broadcast. I agreed, but with one condition. I had to tell the story the Jewish way – the way we have followed for thousands of years when telling the story of the exodus from Egypt. Ancient Jewish teaching specifies that 'one begins with the bad news and ends with the good'. A Jewish story must end on a note of hope. There are no exceptions.

I went, and it was as bad as I expected; worse. There are no words to describe what it feels like to stand on the spot where more than a million Jews – many of them young children – were gassed, burned and turned to dust. I wept uncontrollably in the hall in Stammlager Auschwitz, preserved as a museum, where there was nothing but the recorded voice of a cantor singing *Kel Malei Rachamim*, the traditional Jewish prayer for the dead. A chill shot down my spine as I went from room to room, seeing the piles of objects stripped from the prisoners soon to be dead – the suitcases, clothes, spectacles, artificial limbs, the mountain of shoes. Nothing was too worthless to be saved except one thing – life itself. A million shoes rescued, a million lives thrown away.

It haunted me for months afterwards. It still does from time to time.

It raised many questions in my mind, but the one that was most insistent was the one I never heard anyone ask. What gave the survivors the strength to survive, not then but subsequently? What gave the Jewish people as a whole the courage to continue, knowing as each of us does that, but for an accident of history, we would not have been alive today? What is it that gives life the victory over the angel of death?

The Jewish people did survive and in the past 50 years achieved some of their most monumental creations – the State of Israel, Jerusalem rebuilt, the ingathering of exiles, a series of rescues of threatened Jewries around the world, and a renaissance of Jewish life throughout the Diaspora. I find these things extraordinary, not least for having lived through some of them.

I have met many survivors of the camps, and others who lost entire families there. They still bear the marks of that trauma. How could they not? In many cases it took them 50 years before they could even talk about their memories. Yet I am struck by their passion for life, by their tenacious hold on it. In small ways, and sometimes large, they have worked to build a different world, a world in which such murderous hatreds are no longer possible. Some kept their faith in God, others lost it, but most kept their faith in life itself. They did not give up, or give in to resentment and bitterness, or lapse into the nightmare of victimhood.

Somehow they preserved the lineaments of hope. Nowhere do I find more clearly than in these survivors the difference between optimism and hope. Optimism is the belief that things are going to get better. Hope is the belief that we can make things better. Optimism is a passive virtue, hope an active one. It takes no courage to be an optimist, but it does need courage to hope.

I made my programme the way I wanted to, beginning at Auschwitz but ending in what are for me the two most powerful symbols of Jewish rebirth – Jerusalem and five-year-old children at a new Jewish school, the two homes of the Jewish heart, the places where you see one of the world's most ancient peoples becoming young again.

When Jews speak of life, they do so amidst memories of death. That is why, for me, faith is no simple, naïve, optimistic affirmation. It needs enormous strength, emotional and intellectual, to have faith in the human story.

54

Telling the time

Where does hope come from? It comes from a certain idea about time. So, at any rate, Thomas Cahill argues in his book, *The Gifts of the Jews*. Cahill, a Catholic historian, argues that we owe to the Hebrew Bible one of the great concepts of Western civilization – the idea of linear time. It is in biblical narrative that, for the first time, we encounter the notion that time itself is the setting of the human journey towards a destination – the promised land, the messianic age, the kingdom of heaven. It was this sense of travelling that gave the West its distinctive orientation to the future.

Biblical thought stands in sharp contrast to an earlier vision, the world of myth. The most ancient documents we possess tell of humanity's first attempts to imagine order in societies threatened by natural catastrophe – floods, famines, earthquakes, droughts. These were, or so it seemed, the battles of the gods. The gods themselves were forces of nature. The great drama of myth is the struggle for cosmos against chaos. Its longing is for a world in which stability rules. Time is defined by those things that never change: the movement of the planets, the cycle of the seasons, the eternal recurrence of birth, growth and death. All things return to their source and begin again. Mythical time is cyclical time.

Against this background, few things could have been more revolutionary than the double exodus with which the Bible begins – that of Abraham from Mesopotamia, and that of Moses and the Israelites from Egypt. Biblical faith defines itself in opposition to the two great civilizations of the ancient world. God is no longer to be identified with nature, nor is His image, mankind. Instead we are a fissile mixture of 'dust of the earth' and the 'breath of God'. We speak. We think. We conceptualize. We can imagine a world different from the one that exists. The hierarchies of society are not written into the architecture of the universe. To be human is to be free, capable of choosing between good and evil. If not alone, then in partnership with God and our fellow human beings, we can begin to build a new society, one that honours the equal dignity of all persons as citizens under the sovereignty of God.

Time was transformed. No longer was it essentially static, the preservation of the status quo. Instead it became the stage on which is played the great drama of humanity as it responds, or fails to respond, to the call of God. We are no longer held captive by the past. We are not destined endlessly to repeat our ancestors' mistakes. Our vision is not bounded by what is. A new personality appears: the prophet, the person for whom history is not, in Joseph Heller's words, 'a trash bag of random coincidences torn open in a wind', but instead the long road across the wilderness to freedom. A new emotion is born: hope, the belief that our dreams are not mere waves that break as they reach the hard rocks of reality, that human aspiration is not in vain. Time is the narrative of the human journey, a journey undertaken with hope because, although the way is long and hard, we are not alone.

At some stage, this vision underwent a subtle but fateful change. We cannot date it precisely, but it happened around the seventeenth and eighteenth centuries. Europe had been traumatized by the wars that followed in the wake of the Reformation. People were fighting one another in the name of God – often in the name of the same God. Far from bringing peace, religion seemed to bring conflict. Far from pursuing truth, religion seemed sunk in prejudice which it was prepared tenaciously to defend.

To thoughtful minds, the solution seemed obvious. Secularize politics. Grant religion influence, but not power. Distinguish knowledge from faith. Discover truth through reason and experimentation. Above all, pursue science. The religious vision of man's journey on earth was translated into a secular frame of reference. Old words were given new meanings – words like 'creative', 'civilization', 'improvement', 'evolution' and 'reform'. The term 'modern' which, prior to the eighteenth century, had signalled change in a negative or neutral sense, began to be charged with positive connotations. One word above all others summed up the new consciousness: 'progress', the secular equivalent of linear time.

Progress was the great hope of the Enlightenment. Through science, humanity would conquer ignorance. Through reason, it would banish prejudice. Through trade, it would develop the wealth of nations. Few ideas have had greater simplicity or power. To it we owe the Industrial Revolution, the spread of democracy and the growth of tolerance as an ideal.

Just past the end of the twentieth century, however, our certainties have been shaken. We now know that the Enlightenment failed to prevent the Holocaust. Technology has given us the ability to destroy life on earth. Reason did not cure prejudice. The growth of consumption threatens the environment whose air we breathe. Those who define our present situation as 'postmodernity' are right in one respect. We have lost the simple faith that 'new' necessarily means 'better'. As Robert Bellah put it, 'Progress, modernity's master idea, seems less compelling when it appears that it may be progress into the abyss.'

The answer is not to move backwards. Instead, it is to recall that there was always more than one version of linear time.

There was the Enlightenment narrative of forward motion, driven by science and human rationality. Alongside it, and never wholly eclipsed, was the biblical vision of time as a journey. According to this, the human story is not simple and straightforward. There are setbacks, digressions, wanderings, false turns, but these are not grounds for the death of hope because there is always a sense of destination: the just society, heaven's kingdom, a world of human dignity and grace.

The difference between the two linear narratives is this: progress begets optimism. The religious journey engenders hope. Unlike optimism, hope survives even in tough and confusing times. That is why we need it now.

55

When civilizations grow old

Jean-Jacques Rousseau, that revolutionary of the eighteenth century, was wrong about most things. His work *The Social Contract* was the inspiration for much of the terror of the French Revolution. His *Emile* set education boldly marching off in the wrong direction. Nor does he seem to have been especially admirable in his private life. He had five children by a servant girl, Thérèse Levasseur, and then abandoned them to an orphanage. He had a habit of quarrelling with and then betraying his friends, among them Diderot and Hume. All in all, he seems to have loved humanity rather more than human beings.

Nonetheless, the great writers, and Rousseau was one, always have important things to say. Even when wrong in principle, they are often right in detail. *The Social Contract* contains one riveting paragraph on which it would be hard to improve:

> Nations, like men, are teachable only in their youth; with age they become incorrigible. Once customs are established and prejudices rooted, reform is a dangerous and fruitless exercise; a people cannot bear to see its evils touched, even if only to be eradicated; it is like a stupid, pusillanimous invalid who trembles at the sight of a physician.

For some time now it has been clear that we have been depleting our reserves of moral capital. Our families are fragile. Our communities have grown thin. Our moral intuitions have been shot to pieces by the machine-gun called relativism. These are the very things we need to survive the exhilarating but unsettling times ahead. Families are where we first learn to trust other people. Communities are where we rehearse the virtues we need to build a better world. Moral principles are the compass that helps us navigate the undiscovered country called the future. When these are weak, we become insecure. When they are strong, we can walk with confidence whatever fate brings.

We have to be prepared to change. The trouble is, consistently today we hear the argument that human beings cannot change. 'You can't turn back the tide.' 'Go with the flow.' 'You're dreaming of a golden age that never was.' The family is breaking down? Inevitable. Civility is on the wane? That is how things are. Too much violence in the media? If that is what people want, that is what they get.

None of these is true. Why are they said? Because we have focused on the institutions that reinforce rather than change human behaviour. Governments reflect votes. Politics follows opinion polls. The market mirrors consumer choices. Therapies tell us we are OK as we are.

There is only one thing missing from this constellation. It is the language of aspiration, the idea that whatever we are, we might be different. We *can* grow and develop. We are not simply a bundle of desires. We have immortal longings. That is what gives life its striving. Frankly, it is what gives life its meaning.

It was the Scottish philosopher David Hume who reminded us of the difference between what is and what ought to be. It is that difference that moves us to change the world. People fall ill, so we practise medicine. People suffer, so we provide relief. Western civilization is predicated on the assumption that the evils of this world are not inevitable. Why, then, if we can cure disease, invent technology and transform the environment, can we not alter the way we behave? If we can change everything else, can we not change ourselves? The answer is that we can, but first we have to want to.

That is why religion has such power, and why it will never be eclipsed. Almost alone among the great systems of thought still operative in our time, it sets forth a vision of change – not change at a distance, brought about by governments, scientists or political organizations, but by us in our individual lives and acts. This is change with a human face, a vision of the world in which I have dignity because I can make a difference, as a spouse, a parent, a neighbour, a friend.

Rabbi Yisrael Salanter used to say, 'When I was young, I wanted to change the world. I tried, but the world didn't change. Then I decided to change my town, but the town didn't change. Then I tried to change my family, but my family didn't change. Then I realized: first, I must change myself.'

When a society comes to the collective verdict that it can no longer change, it has reached Rousseau's 'age of incorrigibility'. At that point we have to turn elsewhere, to the institutions that transform because they see not only what we are but also what we might become. That is why faith matters. It is where we keep our aspirations alive. It is where we never relinquish the vision of a better life. It is where we remember that to change the world, first we have to change ourselves. It is the last remaining voice of 'ought' in the midst of 'is'.

56

Surviving change

We are living through an age of change, one of the most dramatic and unpredictable in the history of the world. Hardly a month passes without some breathtaking development in science or technology. The political landscape shifts and reconfigures with bewildering speed. A 'new world order' is in the making, and we do not yet know what it is. The best we can say is: expect the unexpected. Some developments will be benign, others dislocating, but each will be a change, and change is painful. The question is, do we have the resources to deal with it?

Those resources will not primarily be economic, political, scientific or technological. They will be psychological, even spiritual. Coping with change calls for a certain resilience of character. Transition is among the most unsettling things we can face. In one respect, it is harder than war. In war we know, or quickly learn, what to anticipate. In ages of change we confront uncertainty that can last a lifetime. How hard change is, I discovered in an unusual way.

I was making a television documentary on the family, and my research led me to a unit for the treatment of stammering. One speech therapist I had heard about was convinced that families were important in helping children cure their impediment. Her experience had led her to the view that to cure dysfunctions, you had to look not only at the child but also at the whole network of relationships within the family. If you wanted to cure the defect, you also had to renegotiate those relationships.

Working with the parents, she had to find a way of making them realize the difficulty a child faced in breaking a habit. To do this, she made them undergo an experiment. First she told the parents to visualize and describe the object that was most precious to them. Some chose family heirlooms, others their wedding rings. Then she told them to imagine that they had just lost that object and to describe their feelings. They spoke of panic, anger, sadness. It was a kind of bereavement. Then she said, 'Now you know what your child will feel like if it loses its stammer.'

It was a moment of total bewilderment. Until that moment the parents had assumed that their children wanted to be cured. All they needed to do was to learn how. After all, the children knew that they were suffering from a condition that made it hard for them to communicate, form relationships, make friends. But – and this is what none of them had realized until then – the defect had become part of their personalities. They had learned to cope. Their stammer had become part of their self-image. So it was painful for them to change, even though they knew that it would be better for them if they did. We cling to the familiar, even when we know it to be damaging or self-destructive. That is why addiction is so hard to cure. To change, we have to overcome fear. What affects individuals can apply to societies as a whole.

It is not the results of change we need fear, but simply living through them. Nature has marvellous powers of recovery. I vividly remember the hurricane that swept through Southeast England in 1987. We were in the centre of London at the time, and as I walked through Hyde Park and Kensington Gardens at dawn it looked like the end of the world. The roads were strewn with fallen trees. They had crashed through roofs and cars. The great parks, with their formal avenues and gardens, were devastated. A few days later the park keepers started a bonfire to burn the branches and trunks that had blown down. There were so many, the fire lasted for two years. Ten years on, a television documentary traced what had happened since. The groves and forests had all grown back. Those that were left to their own devices had fared even better than the ones that had been deliberately replanted. Nature recovers. So does mankind.

Change is not threatening, so long as we keep firm hold of the values by and for which we live. We can travel with confidence so long as we have a map. We can jump with safety knowing there is someone to catch us as we fall. It is when we lose these things that change creates anxiety. It is when we think that, because technology is changing, our values too must change that we create problems we cannot solve, fear we cannot confront.

57

The Tabernacle

The changes ahead are formidable. No one knows what they will be. As I write, an Internet service provider is about to be floated on the London Stock Exchange. Its valuation? Well in excess of a billion pounds. No one knows whether it will make a profit, and if so, how much and by when and exactly how. Seldom has the hard-edged world of the market been more speculative, more frankly based on guesswork and intuition. How will global communication change the way we live? Will it internationalize culture? Will it force closed societies like China into openness? Will it hasten the end of the nation-state? Will it stabilize or destabilize economies? Will the transferability of production and even clerical tasks mean that all jobs become perennially insecure?

At a more immediate level, will we still shop in stores? Will we continue to work in offices? Will the schools and universities of the future be like they are now? It is perfectly conceivable that within five years a lecturer in Oxford will be able to give a class to students from St Petersburg, Russia to St Petersburg, Florida, and all points in between. They will be able to see him. He will be able to see them. They will send in their essays, and receive them back marked, by e-mail. It will be quicker for them to attend classes than if they were living in Oxford itself. Virtual communities are communities in time, not in space. They are not people in the same room, but people attending to the same thing at the same moment, linked in cyberspace. When institutions change so fundamentally, so do our basic structures of consciousness, and we cannot predict what the results will be. All we know is that we face an age of multiplying uncertainties.

There is a Jewish festival that never fails to move me by its beauty. It is called *Sukkot*, in English, Tabernacles. It takes place at the beginning of autumn, just after the High Holidays are over. Its main feature is the fact that we leave our houses for eight days and instead eat (and in warmer climates sleep) in huts with leaves instead of a roof. They are a reminder of the booths the Israelites lived in for 40 years as they wandered through the desert in search of the promised land. As Jews, we live our history. Although it happened more than 3,000 years ago, we carry it with us, handing it on to our children. There is a difference between living with the past and living in the past. Jews are a forward-looking sort of people. We do not tend to be threatened by technology or science. We embrace it. It is our form of partnership with God, 'perfecting the world' together. Perhaps familiarity with our past gives us confidence in the future. Nothing takes us by surprise. Whatever happens, we have been there before.

Sukkot turned out to be more than an ancient memory. For much of the past 2,000 years it was a compelling symbol of the Jewish present. Scattered, dispersed, without a home or civil rights, Jews found themselves subject to the whims of rulers and popular sentiment, both fickle things in the Middle Ages. Time and again they were uprooted, exiled and expelled. They knew what it was to live under constant uncertainty. However long they had lived in a country and however much they had contributed to its wellbeing, they knew that they or their children might have to uproot themselves and start again, always assuming that they were alive to do so. *Sukkot* was more than a festival. It was the Jewish condition until recent times.

This is why I am in awe of its alternative name, 'The Time of our Joy'. That is what tradition called it, and in so doing it made a momentous affirmation. You can rejoice under conditions of uncertainty, provided you have faith. That faith, as I read it in our sacred writings, was not naïve. It did not assert that all was well with the world. On the contrary, the world was in a state of dislocation and Jews felt it more than most. Nonetheless, God was with them. His presence could be felt in the home, in the tenderness between husband and wife, parent and child, in the warmth of community, the embrace of friends, the support of neighbours. His word lived wherever Jews studied together. And His promise lived, that one day they would see better times. Seldom has a people survived on a more slender hope. But it proved stronger than steel, longer lived than empires. They kept their faith. Their faith kept them.

For me the Tabernacle with its roof of leaves is the symbol of faith. Nothing could be more fragile, vulnerable, open to the wind and rain, a temporary dwelling. Yet nothing sustained a people more than the knowledge that around it were the wings of the Divine presence. The faith of Jews through the generations was not simple, nor was it blind. They had no illusions that all was well in this dark world, yet they sat in the *Sukkah* and sang. To know that life is full of risk and yet affirm it, to sense the full insecurity of the human situation and yet rejoice – that, for me, is faith. It is not about optimism but about courage, the courage to face an unknown future knowing that we are not alone, that God is with us, lifting us when we fall, signalling the way.

Faith: the undiscovered country

Religion today has become a countercultural force. It has been marginalized. Look for religion in the press, and you will find that it is usually the story of a priest or vicar in a sex-scandal case, or it is in the weekend section somewhere between the gardening and travel pages. God has become part of the leisure industry.

This is good news, because it allows us to see it afresh. G. K. Chesterton once planned to write a story about a man who set off to sail to Australia and by accident travelled in a circle and landed on the shores of the country from which he had set off. He did not realize his mistake, and so everything that greeted his eye had the air of the exotic. Home became a foreign country. That is the fate of religion in our time. It has become so old that it is something new. It has been so neglected that we can see it for the first time.

At the heart of faith is not some arcane set of metaphysical propositions that you need a doctorate in theology to understand and naïveté to believe. It is about the dignity of the personal, that strange, unique ability we have to imagine alternative futures, act on the basis of that imagination, and thus begin to change the world. It is about those dimensions of being human that cannot be captured by any scientific theory, because they occupy the realm where cause and effect cease and human creativity begins. Above all, faith is about that quintessential moment when, being self-conscious, we become aware of our solitude and begin to reach out to others through speech and communication. God lives in relationships. The simplest definition of God I can give is the objective reality of the personal. The world responds to us as we respond to the world. Religion is the greatest attempt ever made to endow reality with a human face.

Not by accident is Judaism a religion, less of holy people and holy places than of holy words – the Divine speech, recorded in the Hebrew Bible and endlessly studied ever since. Language is the vehicle of meanings. It is also the primary way in which we form relationships of trust. I 'give my word', meaning that I use language to create an obligation which I am thereby bound to honour. The Hebrew word for faith – *emunah* – really means honouring your word and trusting others to honour theirs. Above all, language is where we frame our values, express our ideals, and thus create the possibility of a gracious society. It allows us to have a vision and communicate it. 'Without a vision,' says the proverb, 'a people perish.' Civilizations fail when they forget what they were striving for, and that is what ours is beginning to do.

Science, politics and economics, the three great forces of our world, are impersonal. That is their strength. Were they personal, they would fail. Science would become myth. Politics would become nepotism. Economics would become the trading of favours. It is also their weakness, however, for there is something about being human that they will never capture – what it is to be me, with these hopes, aspirations, dreams and fears. The great virtue of art is that it deals with the personal, but art is not life. It is life caught, framed, frozen, dramatized, exhibited, but not life lived. That is why religion is uniquely powerful, because it takes the personal and turns it into living structures that honour personhood – families, communities, narratives, rituals, traditions, customs, holy times, prayers. The great religious institutions are a sustained celebration of the personal – not of individuality, but of persons in relation held together by the overarching personhood of God.

We need it now. An impersonal world can be one in which there is fun, escapism, fantasy and the satisfaction of desire. We can take Prozac or other drugs to neutralize the pain, but we cannot achieve happiness. Happiness is what we make with others when we honour them as persons and strive for ideals that others share. An impersonal world, dominated by states and markets, large corporations and global forces, is one where each of us is replaceable, none of us valued for what we uniquely are. It fails to speak to our deepest needs as social, meaning-seeking animals. We are persons. That is the most fundamental thing about us, and it is in structures that honour the dignity of the personal that happiness lies.

Religion is at its best when it becomes a countercultural force; when it has no power, only influence, no authority except that which it earns, no claim to people's attention other than by the way it creates values that cannot be found elsewhere. It is then that it loses its perennial tendency to corruption and becomes again what it once was – a startling new voice, redeeming us from our loneliness, framing our existence with meaning, and teaching us to remember what so much else persuades us to forget – that the possibilities of happiness are all around us, if we would only open our eyes and give thanks.